Who Am I?

A Novel of Fantasy, Family Bonds, and Self-Discovery

Donald Schmit

Who Am I? A Novel of Fantasy, Family Bonds, and Self-Discovery

Donald Schmit

Published by 1st World Publishing
P.O. Box 2211, Fairfield, Iowa 52556
tel: 641-209-5000 • fax: 866-440-5234
web: www.1stworldpublishing.com

First Edition

ISBN Softcover: 978-1-4218-3584-6

LCCN: Library of Congress Cataloging-in-Publication Data

This material has been written and published for educational purposes to enhance one's well-being. In regard to health issues, the information is not intended as a substitute for appropriate care and advice from health professionals, nor does it equate to the assumption of medical or any other form of liability on the part of the publisher or author. The publisher and author shall have neither liability nor responsibility to any person or entity with respect to loss, damages, or injury claimed to be caused directly or indirectly by any information in this book.

Part I:
Hidden World

Chapter 1

Chasing Dreams, Living Reality

"Alexi Ann!"

The soft scribble of pens and the shuffle of paper was cut short.

Startled from her daydream atop an Olympic podium, Alexi looked up to meet her eighth-grade teacher's knowing gaze. A few curious heads swiveled, momentarily distracted from their history worksheets. Suki, Alexi's loyal friend, flashed a reassuring smile from the next desk.

Ms. Cheesman didn't reprimand. Instead, her hands moved through the air, gathering an imaginary deck of cards, slipping them into their case, and sliding them into her desk drawer. Her mime wasn't lost on Alexi. With a resigned sigh, she followed suit, stowing away her treasured cards honoring the USA Olympic women's softball champions. She glanced one last time at the gold medal on the card case before tucking it into her bag.

Ms. Cheesman's lips moved silently, forming words. Alexi wondered, *Can a mime use their mouth? Seems like it's against the rules.* But the message was unmistakable: stick around after class.

The quiet hum of the classroom resumed, but Alexi's mind was already on tomorrow's regional semifinal. Her fingers were itching to grip the softball, her heart swelling with pride for the Olympic women who won gold three times in a row.

The clang of the bell snapped Alexi back to reality. She turned to Suki, exchanged a hand slap, a giggle, and their customary Friday declaration, "That's history."

Wonder what Cheesy has in mind this time, she thought as she walked to the front of the classroom.

"Alexi, you realize this is American History, not the History of Women's Softball. Right?" Ms. Cheesman scolded.

No duh. Alexi almost blurted out, but she bit her tongue.

Ms. Cheesman, calm and composed, looked directly at her. "I'm baffled. You're bright but barely manage a C in this class. And please—no more cute answers on tests."

Alexi stood silently as Ms. Cheesman rifled through a folder, pulling out the previous day's test. "Who was Thomas Jefferson's closest confidant?" she read. "Your answer: *Who cares?*"

Her cheeks flushed. "Sorry, I didn't know the answer."

Ms. Cheesman's expression softened, though her voice remained firm. "Leave it blank next time—please. I see two sides of you, Alexi. Last week, when Ronni was having a bad day and started crying, you sat beside her and put your arm around her. Not many kids would do that. And the time…"

Ms. Cheesman paused mid-sentence as she saw Alexi gaze toward the open door.

"Okay, better not miss your bus! Off you go. And good luck tomorrow. Half the school will be there—including me," Ms. Cheesman's voice trailed her out the door.

A smile crossed Alexi's lips as she thought about acknowledging her teacher's support. Instead, she lowered her head and sprinted down the hall to catch her bus, sliding into the seat next to Suki as the door closed.

Alexi caught her breath and turned to Suki. "You know, Cheesy's pretty good with that mime stuff. Almost makes getting into trouble worth it. And for a teacher, she's not half bad. Sometimes I feel bad about the dead mouse Ricky and I put in her desk drawer last semester. I don't know why we did that. But *Cheesman*—what a name to get stuck with, eh? But what can you do?"

"Get married," Suki quipped with her trademark deadpan delivery.

Alexi grinned. "You think someone would marry her? Bet she's never even kissed anyone." They giggled, leaning closer, proud of their sense of maturity.

"Wanna go to the mall after the game tomorrow?"

Suki frowned. "Can't. Mom wants me to go to the library to go over my English lessons so I can speak, spoke, spoken better."

"But Saturday? Seriously?"

"Mom no care only daughter have fun," Suki said, mimicking her mother's uncompromising tone. "Japanese moms don't take Saturdays off, and neither do their kids."

"Ugh... fine."

Suki put on her headset while Alexi flipped through her notebook. She settled on a page decorated with the carefully crafted letters ICAL. After adding a few flourishes, she held it in front of Suki and mouthed the words *In Mr. Eddy's class*. Suki got it. She knew Alexi had been working on the design for a month, and only the two of them knew it meant "I care a lot." The irony wasn't lost on Suki—their inside joke was that Alexi didn't actually care about anything—except softball.

Alexi flipped to the poem section in her notebook and quickly became absorbed as the bus rumbled down the street.

"Aleeeeexi?" The bus driver's voice rang through the bus, stretching her name into a playful jab.

"Jerkoid," Alexi muttered. "What's with her? She sounds like the brakes on steroids."

"Maybe she's auditioning for the world's most unimpressed

audience," Suki quipped. They laughed as they exchanged their secret handshake.

Alexi grabbed her backpack, notebook in hand, and rushed toward the door. Rushing down the aisle, she tripped over Roger's extended legs—an occurrence that was becoming all too familiar. She looked at him, uncertain of her feelings. He offered a sheepish shrug, as if to say, *Oops, sorry, I didn't see you.* Roger was the eighth-grade basketball star, class president, and the only classmate taller than her.

She glanced at Suki, who smirked. *Told you Roger liked you.* Alexi wasn't sure how to react. She bolted off the bus, leaving the puzzle of Roger and her feelings for another day.

Walking up the sidewalk to her house, she flipped through her notebook to three poems she wrote at school. Suki gave her a haiku book for Christmas; its succinct form had inspired her ever since.

All life rolled up into one small softball. She looked at the next one: *If I were beautiful, would I still be me?* A smile started to form, then faded. She read the last one: *Time imprisons me to a sentence of hopeless boredom.* She chuckled at the play on words as she skipped through the front door. Her cat scurried off, flicking its tail in annoyance as the door slammed shut. She headed to the kitchen, dropped her backpack on the floor, grabbed a jug of grape juice from the fridge, and gulped.

Footsteps echoed from the hallway as her mother, Mira, appeared in the doorway, staring at the floor.

"Alexi Ann!" Her voice was sharp.

"What?" *There's that Ann again. I wonder if Mom gave me a middle name so I'd know when I'm in trouble.*

Mira pointed to a squashed caterpillar that unfortunately came between Alexi and the fridge.

"It's just a bug," she said, playfully dragging her foot across the goo. She noticed that the green smear matched the color of her sneakers and grinned.

"Not funny. Now clean it up."

With a sigh, Alexi grabbed a sponge and wiped the traces of the caterpillar from the floor. She tossed the sponge in the sink, wiped her hands on her jeans, and sprinted to her room two stairs at a time.

Chapter 2

Daydreams and Curveballs

Beep, beep, beep.

Alexi slapped off the alarm, sprang out of bed, and swept her long blond hair into a loose ponytail. She dashed to the bathroom, splashed water on her face, and caught a crooked smirk in the mirror. Her blue eyes flickered with curiosity, as if searching for something just out of reach. Beneath her restless energy lived an old soul, the kind that draws people in without trying.

Last year's City Champs uniform felt tighter in all the wrong places, a reminder of her recent growth spurt. With a fist pump and a grin, she bolted downstairs, game-day adrenaline already kicking in.

She stared at her breakfast, aimlessly pushing the food around her plate, her mind running through pitching strategies for batters she would soon face.

"Please don't play with your food," Mira's voice interrupted her musing.

"Okay," Alexi muttered, then glanced at her father, hunched over a crossword puzzle. "Dad, are you coming to the game next Saturday?"

He looked up, only half hearing the question. "Huh? Oh, sorry dear, but the guys have a fishing trip planned at Ray's cabin, and..."

"But if we win today, it's the final next Saturday. I'll be the starting pitcher..." She tilted her head toward her plate, realizing it was a lost cause. In her mind, though, she was already on the mound. She scanned the bleachers, saw her mom's excited wave, and next to her—a big fish. She scrunched her face.

Her dad's voice drifted back in, soft and apologetic: "Really sorry, dear..." But she was already lost in the game, her family's presence, both here and not, blending into the background.

"Just a little OJ before you head out?" Mira offered gently.

Alexi took a quick sip, rushed upstairs for her softball cap, and darted out the door as Mira's reminder, "Don't forget to take out the…" trailed off behind her.

The door slammed behind her, echoing through the house. Outside, her bike tires crunched on the gravel as she rode away.

Mira turned to Benjamin, who was absently scratching his chin with a pencil, pondering a nine-letter word for sleepy. Suddenly, she blurted, "Sometimes I don't know what to do with that girl. I try not to be overbearing and critical, but I also don't want to ignore inappropriate behavior. Whatever I do, I don't feel good about it."

"The dean of my department says that repeating the same actions will likely lead to the same results," Benjamin responded in his usual calm tone.

* * *

The weekend of the finals had finally arrived. Alexi raced downstairs in her crisply pressed softball uniform, still buzzing from last week's 11-2 win. Her pitches, many over 55 MPH, allowed only one batter to reach first. Her coach's decision to replace her after four innings with the second-string pitcher seemed an act of mercy rather than a strategy.

"Alexi," Mira said softly. "Didn't you notice how dark it is outside? I'm sorry, but Betty called and said a 'fickle weather pattern' developed overnight, with rain and lightning predicted for today, so your game's been postponed." She paused, then mused, "A fickle weather pattern? Never heard that one before."

Alexi's eyes drifted to the window and whispered an almost inaudible expletive.

"Alexi Ann!" Mira raised her voice in surprise.

"Why does this always happen to me?" Alexi's voice quivered, hovering just below a shout.

"Always?" Mira asked gently.

"Yes, everything sucks."

"Alexi Ann!" Mira, ever the beacon of open-mindedness, still winced at her daughter's choice of expressions. Alexi flopped onto the couch, hating her middle name, as dejection settled over her like a storm cloud.

Mira's voice softened again as she reached out to comfort her. "I know it feels that way. We all have those days. But hey, Dad's off fishing with his friends—a little rain won't stop them—so it's just us girls. I've got some cleaning to do, but I have a surprise for you afterward."

Alexi scowled. "A surprise? What, like cleaning my room?"

"If I tell you, it won't be a surprise, will it?" Mira said with a sly smile.

Alexi huffed and shuffled to her room. "Yeah, sure. Whatever."

A couple of hours later, Mira knocked on her door and, after a pause, entered. "How are things in the dugout?" she asked lightly.

Alexi's room teetered on the edge of chaos. Softball posters lined the dark teal walls—the largest celebrating the 2000 USA women's Olympic gold medal softball team. Nearby, a photo captured a proud moment from the previous year's seventh-grade volleyball season—Alexi in mid-air, blocking a shot.

"I'm so bored," Alexi groaned, idly spinning a softball in her hand. "Why do things always go wrong for me?"

Mira sat beside her, speaking softly. "Life isn't all good all the time for anyone. I know you're disappointed about your game, but what else do you want besides softball?"

Alexi rolled her eyes, as if what she needed to be happy should be obvious to everyone. "All right, I'll tell you. I want a big house with a pool, like Lilly's—and a horse. I want to be able to go to the library instead of sitting in Mr. Eddy's snore-fest class. I don't want to be so freaky tall, and this straight hair has to go. I want to be the best pitcher in our town—no, our state—and…"

Mira's voice was gentle but carried a hint of strategy. "So, you're not happy with who you are. Right?"

Alexi rolled her eyes again, this time adding a sarcastic "Duh."

"Remember when I used to read stories to you?"

With a sigh, Alexi gave a half-hearted nod.

"A couple of weeks ago, this book came in the mail. Odd thing, I don't recall ordering it." Mira pressed forward, her fingers tracing caricatures on the cover. "How about I read it to you like old times?"

"Oh, Mom, that's so yesterday. I'm way past story time."

"Okay, here's the deal," Mira bargained, "listen for a half-hour, and then you're free to bail."

"But Mom…"

Unfazed, Mira soldiered on, "If you agree, you're off the hook for kitchen duty tonight. Plus, I've got a batch of your favorite chocolate brownies waiting for dessert."

"Brownies after the fish dinner Dad's bringing home?" Alexi surrendered with a half-smile.

"Dad's home on Sunday, so no fish fry tonight. We should be thankful his day job isn't fishing, or we'd starve."

Alexi cracked a smile.

* * *

Mira sat on the couch downstairs, the book resting on her lap. Across from her, Alexi slouched in the recliner, doing her best to mask her curiosity behind a wall of teenage indifference.

"Want to sit closer so you can see the pictures?" Mira patted the cushion next to her.

"Nah, I'm good. What's it about?" Alexi asked, barely lifting her eyes.

"White blood cells," Mira said, looking at Alexi, anticipating her reaction.

Alexi's face scrunched, her voice rising an octave. "Mom! Seriously? Just because you're a doctor—white blood cells? Mom!"

Mira grinned, a playful glint in her eye. "Oh, it's not just about white blood cells. It's also about bacteria, antibodies, and germs."

Alexi sank deeper into the recliner, sighing loudly as her mom opened the book and read the author's introduction.

> This is the story of Arlo and Zoe—just two of the trillions of white blood cells inside every person reading this book.

"Or listening," Mira added, glancing at a groaning Alexi before continuing the introduction.

> Our bodies teem with white blood cells, enzymes, and antibodies, all working together in unseen harmony to digest food and combat diseases.
>
> I've taken the liberty of reimagining this microscopic realm as the home of our storybook heroes, Arlo and Zoe—cells

in a body who live, learn, and progress much like humans. In their cellular world, you'll find houses, families, and schools just like ours. So, let your imagination take the reins, and prepare to look, listen, learn, and...

Mira turned to Alexi, drawing out the last word with a grin: "*DREAM.*"

Chapter 3

Arlo and Zoe

Mira turned to the first chapter and began reading, weaving science and imagination together with a lighthearted touch.

Arlo slouched at the dinner table, the weight of being nineteen—in white blood cell years—pressing on him.

"How was school today, son?" His dad, a veteran of life's struggles, asked.

"Fine," he muttered.

"I know what *fine* means," his dad prodded. "It's cell-speak for 'I don't want to talk about it,' right?"

Arlo barely shrugged.

"What's up? Bad day?"

"You wouldn't understand."

His dad leaned forward. "Try me."

Arlo sighed. "It's just… I mean... I'm graduating in a few weeks, and everyone except me knows what they're going to do."

Across the table, his mother chimed in, "You can get a job like your father."

Arlo's voice sharpened. "I don't want to live this kind of life."

"What kind of a life do you want?" his dad asked.

His face tightened, "I don't know, but not like... not like this." He gestured around the room. "Tyson's house is a mansion, and he can do whatever he wants. Why can't you be like... I'm not hungry." He pushed back his chair and stormed to his room.

"Arlo!" His mom called after him. She turned to her husband, "I can't believe that kid, after all we..."

"Joyce, it's okay. He'll be fine. I was rebellious at that age too. Not exactly like that, but I guess it's part of growing up. I remember hearing Dad tell my mom, 'Seems like as soon as you realize your parents weren't so bad, you have kids who think you are.'"

* * *

Arlo's pencil traced the loops and turns of the human digestive system as his brows furrowed in concentration. A page slipped loose and drifted to the floor, barely noticed in the busy study hall. Sitting next to him, Zoe picked it up, glanced at it, and handed it back with a curious smile.

After school, Zoe picked up her guitar from the cramped storage closet and set off for home. On her way, she bumped into Arlo.

"You play?" he asked, nodding toward the guitar case.

"A little. Mostly write songs." She tapped a rhythm on her case. "You?"

"I did," he grinned. "Drums. *The Crazy Hatter Band*. We broke up. Heard of us?"

She shook her head, her steps syncing with his. "Nah. I'm

new here." After a few more steps, she playfully asked, "So you're trading drums for travel?"

He blinked, caught off guard. "Travel? What?"

"I saw your map in study hall. Hard to travel with drums strapped to your back," Zoe teased, glancing at his notebook.

His cheeks flushed as he quickly tucked the stray papers back inside.

"It's okay. I'm all for it," she assured him. "Who wouldn't want more than this?" she asked, gesturing around them at the cramped, tubular structure they were walking through. "But your map… it's kind of small, don't you think?"

His eyes widened.

"There's a lot more out there," she said, a hint of mystery in her voice.

"And how would you know?" he challenged.

"I've been around," she smiled slyly, "Just saying."

Arlo pulled out his diagram with a trace of pride. "More than this?"

"We study the digestive system because that's where we live, but there are tons of other…"

"Yeah, right," he cut in.

She pressed on. "I don't think you'll believe me, but I'm not from here. I used to live in another host."

"Another host?" he chuckled.

"Yep, another host, another human—my former world." Her voice turned wistful.

They spotted a park bench a few blocks from the school. As they settled onto it, he teased, "If it were me, I'd put a 'g' in front of host."

Zoe snickered. "Here's what happened. My friend Karen told

me she had taken an amazing journey and saw everything."

"Everything?" Arlo's curiosity piqued.

"If you saw what I did, you'd know there's more than that." She pointed to his notebook. He nodded, encouraging her to continue, wondering if she was about to broaden his horizons for his upcoming adventure.

"When Karen first told me about her journey, I was skeptical," Zoe admitted. "But curiosity got the best of me. I asked her to take me, and she led me into a world I never knew existed."

Zoe recounted her trip with Karen, squeezing through tight spaces and gliding through veins and muscles. "When we reached the retina, an astonishing new reality came into view. It was... eye-opening. Just saying."

Arlo exhaled a faint 'hmm.' "Okay, you got my attention. You saw what?"

"Outside my world," Zoe said, her excitement building, "to a realm that was unbelievably cool. Karen told me we were in the host's eye—a human is what they call themselves—and it was our lucky day. This human was looking into a mirror, brushing her teeth. We didn't see her, just her reflection. Then, another human appeared beside her, and they started talking. The whole scene felt surreal."

She paused to gauge Arlo's reaction as her story took on new layers.

"We were inside Tara's eye, and the other person was Eric. He was talking about a new Italian restaurant his friend recommended. Tara voiced concerns, but Eric assured her that all was fine because of his new cholesterol meds. Before his reflection disappeared, he kissed her. After Tara finished her makeup, she flashed Karen and me a big smile and a satisfying wink."

Zoe finished her tale and noticed that Arlo was now leaning forward on the bench. "As soon as Tara disappeared, Karen and I skedaddled back home. The way they were talking, it seems like there are lots of those things out there,"

"Lots of...um…hosts?" he asked.

She shrugged. "Guess so."

He blinked. "Wait—So we're inside Tara?"

"Nope. We're in Eric. He's my host now, too. Kinda creepy, right?"

Arlo leaned back slowly, trying to take it in. "Eric?"

"While I was in Tara, I went to a school where we learned about the host's systems—respiration, circulation, that kind of stuff. But here… it's more like a trade school—just the digestive system. One day, while we were studying the function of lips, of all things, I felt a sudden surge. Everything changed. My family, Karen—gone."

Arlo shook his head. "I'm still not on your wavelength."

"I only figured it out because I saw them kiss. That's how I got transferred into this host. And I'm sure it's Eric. When I first got here, I made the trip a few times, and once, I saw Eric in his bedroom mirror."

Arlo's eyes widened. "What does Eric look like?"

"There's no way I can describe it. You'll have to see for yourself."

"Freaky," he muttered. "But that doesn't mean I believe you."

"I hardly believe it myself," Zoe admitted, "but seeing that changed my life. When we go on our walkabout, I'll show you how it's done."

"We? We?"

Chapter 4

An Unexpected Duo

After a quick fridge break, Alexi returned with a soda, and Mira resumed reading.

The scent of dinner permeated the air as Arlo burst through the door. His mom, still in her white cell uniform, looked up from sorting the mail and smiled. "Arlo, would you be a sweetheart and take these letters to Mr. Hershel? His mail ended up in our box again."

Arlo was all in. "Sure, Mom!" he replied, grabbing the letters. Visiting Mr. Hershel always meant fascinating stories. He bolted out the door and headed to the house across the street.

Mr. Hershel opened the door even before Arlo knocked. "Hello, Mr. Hershel," Arlo said, handing over the letters.

"Thanks, Arlo," Mr. Hershel said, glancing at the mail. "Your dad still at work?"

Arlo nodded. "Mind if I ask you something?"

Mr. Hershel smiled and gestured with a 'be my guest' wave.

"I've been wondering what you did before you retired."

Mr. Hershel smiled again and invited Arlo into his finely

decorated home. "Well, as you know, I'm a red blood cell. My job was to manage the delivery of oxygen to various parts of our host, sort of like how a mailman delivers letters," he chuckled, holding up his mail. "I hope I did it better than this."

"Hosts are real?" Arlo asked, wondering why he had never thought much about it before.

"Absolutely," Mr. Hershel confirmed.

"I've heard about hosts. But what exactly is a host?" Arlo asked.

"It's a human, Arlo. We're all human-helpers—your dad, me, you. Our job is to keep our host healthy and happy."

Arlo's thoughts were swirling, "So they're happy, but what about us? Can we be happy too?"

"I know I am," he declared. "And I can tell you someone else who's happy."

"Who?"

"Your father," he said softly.

"My dad?" Arlo's voice spiked. The idea felt about as likely as a virus signing a peace treaty.

"Indeed, your dad," Mr. Hershel insisted. "But I wasn't always content. There was a time when life was a blur—working like crazy for more of everything. Don't get me wrong, I'm not against hard work and reaching for the stars, but there's more to life than how much we can accumulate."

"Wow! Sounds like becoming happy takes a lot of work."

"I had to work hard at not working hard," Mr. Hershel chuckled. "The only way to truly understand this is to go out and discover it for yourself."

Typically uninterested in parental advice, especially from his father, he found pearls of wisdom in Mr. Hershel's words.

Just then, Mrs. Hershel popped around the corner with a tray of cookies. "Oh dear, don't put ideas like that into the boy's head," she said, gently scolding.

Mr. Hershel chuckled as he scribbled across his notepad. "Ever since you were young, I knew you'd have to figure things out for yourself. Your dad told me you're planning a walkabout after graduation."

Arlo caught his breath. "What? Who told him?"

"Parents sometimes know more than you think. If you get to the heart…" he said, handing Arlo the note.

"The heart?" Arlo echoed.

"You'll figure it out. Give this note to Mr. Wattles—the heart's chief engineer. A lot's going on out there—and in here." He tapped Arlo's chest and winked. As Arlo turned to leave, Mr. Hershel added, "There's more to the heart than just a pumping station. One day, you'll discover what that is."

* * *

A few days later, Arlo and his dad were strolling toward his workplace. "Been a while since you've seen the place, huh? Not much has changed. We've got a new sign on our building. I guess that's something."

Arlo looked up at the sign: *Elmer & Sons Antibody Factory*. Unlike the other letters, the last 's' was bright white with crisp edges. He grinned, nudging his dad. "Looks like Elmer finally had another son, huh?"

His dad smiled. "I wouldn't have asked you to come, but it's required for your last week of classes."

"Yeah, I know," Arlo replied.

"You'll have to stay on the observation deck," his dad

gestured toward the raised platform. "See you for lunch."

Arlo headed up the industrial stairs, cautiously avoiding the sticky globs of mucus dotting them. Reaching the deck, he scanned the scene below— machines churned out Y-shaped units, which slid into carts and then vanished into tubes marked Bloodstream. His focus shifted as a limping figure appeared. Smitty, judging by his name tag, took a seat next to him.

"You all right?" Arlo asked.

"Dang cart nabbed my foot," Smitty grunted, nodding towards the Emergency Waiting Area sign. "You?"

"My dad," he pointed downstairs.

Smitty smirked slightly. "Oh, yeah, a school thing,"

Arlo's eyes settled on Smitty's shirt, which sported a diagram of the intestines with the caption: The bulk doesn't stop here. He chuckled. "Been around, huh?"

Smitty glanced down at his shirt, pleased someone noticed. "Sure have. Flew the coop a few years ago. Wanted to see what's out there. Almost got eaten by a dang tapeworm. This big!" He stretched out his arms like it was a prize-winning fish. "Yessiree, I've been places."

"How was it? The traveling?" Arlo asked.

"Tough at times, but the best thing I ever done. You thinkin' of breakin' outta here?"

"Maybe… kinda," his voice trailing off.

"Where ya goin'?

"I don't know. I've heard there's a lot more out there than just this." Arlo stretched his arms to invisible horizons.

"Oh yeah, more an' you can shake a tail feather at!" Smitty said, grateful for the distraction. "Anywhere's better than this dead-end factory."

"Ever been to the heart?" Arlo asked, hesitating. "I've been thinking…"

"Nah," he waved dismissively. "Waste of time. Bunch of fuddy-duddies up there. Couldn't get in with a sledgehammer."

Arlo hesitated. "My neighbor gave me sort of a pass."

Smitty raised his eyebrows. "No joke? Tried getting into that joint myself."

"You know the way?" Arlo perked up.

"Sure do. It's a rush just gettin' there. You'll see." Smitty laughed, sketching a rough map on a napkin. "So, who's your plus one?"

"I'm not going with anyone," Arlo answered, attempting bravado.

"Ouch, that could be a little crazy," Smitty said, wincing.

"Crazy? Why?"

"I gotta tell ya, there's a sea of them…" Smitty's words were cut short as his number flashed on the appointment screen. "Whoa, looks like I'm the chosen one! Here's a map of sorts. Goin' solo, huh?" he uttered incredulously as he headed to the nurse, leaving Arlo with a map he could hardly read and a whirlpool of newfound doubts.

Chapter 5

Fact or Fiction

Mira glanced at her watch, then slipped a bookmark from her 'favorites' basket into the book. "Looks like it's time for lunch. Want to continue after we eat?"

"Yeah, sure. I guess," Alexi said, slowly returning to reality, her mind was lingering on whether Arlo would make it to the heart.

"I read the book already, so I know some scary parts are coming up," Mira teased with a smile as they made their way to the kitchen. Soon, the comforting aroma of grilled cheese sandwiches and tomato soup filled the air. Alexi set the table and poured two glasses of juice.

"I was thinking, blood cells aren't real, right?" Alexi asked.

"What makes you think they aren't? That caterpillar may have thought it was real, but never considered us as real. 'Real' is a point of view. However, what all animals, plants, and white blood cells have in common is life. We all live together on this planet."

"Yeah, I know cells don't have hands and feet, like the pictures in the book, but..."

"But they do have DNA," Mira said, "and just like us—and

that poor crunched caterpillar—cells don't want to die. The body contains both helpful and harmful cells and bacteria. Arlo and Zoe are good cells, helping when you get a cold or the flu. Before becoming a doctor, I had no idea there were millions of human-helpers inside our mouths. Did you brush your teeth this morning?"

"Uh... well..."

"Okay, then millions of bacteria," Mira said, suppressing a grin. They settled down to eat, and Mira continued, "White blood cells are the unsung heroes of our immune system. They play an oversized role in maintaining our health. Can you bring me the grocery list on the fridge?"

Alexi grabbed the whiteboard and handed it to her mom. Mira shifted her plate aside, erased the list, and sketched a diagram.

"Arlo's dad is a white blood cell whose job is to detect harmful germs like bacteria and viruses that enter the body. When someone with the flu sneezes at school, germs float into the air. When you breathe them in, they multiply and attack your healthy cells." Mira said, blending fact with flair, keeping it light.

"His dad works at a factory that produces helpers called antibodies, which look like the Ys in the book. The Y antibody turns upside down and caps the germ, deactivating the harmful part. It's like how neutering our cat stopped him from causing trouble."

"But the flu got me, didn't it?" Alexi asked, her spoon hovering over her bowl.

"When you're not in tip-top health, the good guys inside you have a lot to handle, and sometimes, the germs might score a win. But here's the cool part. Each battle, win or lose, makes your immune system smarter and stronger. Your cells actually 'remember' the next time you have an infection or disease. It's like playing softball against a tough team. Whether you win or lose, every game makes you a better player."

"So that book is kinda real?"

Mira chuckled, "Yes, kinda."

After finishing her meal, Alexi took her plate to the sink. A tattered photo stuck to the fridge caught her eye.

"What's this? I don't remember seeing it before."

Mira glanced over. "I put it there a few days ago. It's a little reminder for me."

Intrigued, Alexi removed it from the fridge and examined it. It was a photo of her mom and Grandma Alice in full hippie regalia. Her mom, just eight, was dressed like a Native American, while Alice wore a tie-dyed, flared-sleeve dress over bell-bottoms—*Love* and *Peace* painted down each leg. "I can't believe you two looked like this."

Gazing into the distance, Mira agreed softly, "Neither can I. Neither can I."

Alexi flipped the photo over and noticed stains on the back. "It looks ancient, Mom."

"Well, duh," Mira teased. Alexi giggled at an expression she'd never heard her mom use before. She read the quote on the back of the picture.

Love is gentle and yet strong and persistent.
Like water, it wears through to the hardest of hearts.
Love and keep on loving, and watch the way open up.
And never accept no for an answer.

– Eileen Caddy.

"Sounds ridonkulous."

"Are they teaching the Queen's English in school now?" Mira asked raising an eyebrow. "You know, I found that picture while flipping through an old book. It made me realize how much I've lost touch with how I felt when I was your age. That quote was my favorite when I wrote it on the back."

"In your flower days, huh?" Alexi grinned.

"Yep. Want to continue reading?"

Alexi settled on the couch next to her mom in the living room. "So I can see the pictures," she explained.

Mira opened the book with a smile. "Okay, we left off after Smitty." The world around them faded as they dove back into the unfolding tale.

Chapter 6

The Adventure Begins

"Hey, Arlo, getting ready to skip town?" Zoe needled, catching him a few days before the end of the school year.

What makes you think that?" He replied cautiously.

"Classes are done in a couple of days. Whatcha gonna do? Just hang?" She prodded, nudging him with her elbow.

Arlo hesitated. "I've been thinking..."

Zoe gasped, "Real thoughts? Whoa!"

"Seriously. You've been around, Right? So, I was wondering..."

"Ready when you are," she cut in, grinning slyly. "Always up for a new adventure and no family ties here. You?"

He'd never taken such a leap before. His gut protested, but he shook it off and said confidently, "School's over in three days. Then we go, okay? But if you can't keep up…"

"Got it," Zoe agreed, extending her little finger for a pinky promise. Their faces lit up with excitement as their fingers interlocked, sealing the deal.

Arlo smiled with a sense of relief now that the decision had finally been made. "Ever been to the heart?"

"No, but I've heard that place is off-limits."

"Maybe, maybe not," he said, proudly showing her the letter from Mr. Hershel and the map from Smitty, recounting his conversations with both.

"Oh, so you need protection!" she smirked.

Arlo's cheeks flushed red.

"Just saying," she grinned with mock innocence.

* * *

A few days later, Arlo and Zoe squeezed their way through the twisting passages of their host's stomach.

"Wow, this place is like a maze," Zoe muttered, her eyes darting from one tunnel to another. "Not sure which one to take. We don't want to get lost—or do we?"

"How about the red one?" Arlo suggested. "Looks good as any in this mess."

She nodded. "Let's do it!"

They followed the tunnel as it twisted and turned before coming face-to-face with a foreboding sign: *Enter at your Own Risk—Liver Under Reconstruction*.

Arlo hesitated, "What the...? This feels wrong."

"We're in a one-way tunnel, so let's make a go of it," Zoe said, sounding brave beyond the circumstances. "It looks like an exit tunnel over there." Her optimism faded as that option quickly evaporated, and they were swept forward by a crowd of cells, deeper into the unknown. Suddenly, they were jettisoned into a dense reddish-black glob.

"Well, we're here… or somewhere," she mused, taking in their gloomy surroundings. "Compared to this, our homes are mansions."

Their feet sank into the ground, pulling at them like quicksand. Arlo groaned, "We have to get out of here." As they trudged forward, he spotted a gleam of light. "Hey. Looks like a guard station."

They made their way to a rundown shack where a lone figure lounged by the door. Zoe flashed a quick smile. "Hi, I'm Zoe, and this is Arlo. Mind if we ask you something?"

"Sure, I'm on a break, ask away. Name's Max."

"Great! Can you tell us what goes on here?"

Max spread his arms wide, nodding. "Welcome to the liver, aka *The Recycling Plant*. We handle the stomach's leftovers, sort through the mess, and send the junk packing." He gestured towards a sign: *To the Intestines*.

"What about the not junk, the usable stuff?" Zoe asked.

"Oh, the tasty morsels? That takes a different route." He pointed to another sign: To the Kidneys. "It's a bit more complicated, but that's the gist of how we roll here."

"Why is it so dark and depressing?" Arlo asked.

Max's smile faded, "Ah, that's a sad tale. Our host is struggling, and it's taken a toll on my crew. Once, these halls were rich reddish-brown, so clean we could bounce off the walls. Now? See for yourself. Anyway, we're starting to see some improvement. That's the short of it. Any more questions, and I'll have to charge you by the minute." A playful chuckle brightened his face.

Grateful, Arlo and Zoe thanked him as he pointed them toward the exit. Arlo couldn't resist dragging his finger along the wall as they slogged out. "This place is bizarre. Feels like squishy, rubbery muck. Definitely needs a scrub."

"Or Eric could lay off the Italian restaurants," Zoe interjected. Her expression turned serious. "Arlo, I keep thinking about

Mr. Hershel's suggestion about visiting the heart."

"I'm with you on that," Arlo agreed.

"Can we make a small detour first?" Zoe's eyes met Arlo's with a subtle plea. "I'm missing my guitar. I left it in my room. We're not far from there."

"Sure, no problem. Then it's onward to the heart!" Arlo struck an over-the-top superhero pose, fist thrust forward. It was goofy, but Zoe burst into laughter.

"Let's check out this one-way passage," Zoe gestured. "Must be what Max was talking about. It's a squeeze, but I think we can do it."

Before they could catch their breath, a new surge of cells swept them into the tunnel. They tumbled through, crashing into a snug gap where they found themselves crammed closely together, a bit too together for Arlo's comfort.

"Oops, sorry, I didn't mean to..." Arlo stammered once they reached the other end.

Zoe shrugged it off with a smile, "No worries."

Arlo's mind was racing with emotions he couldn't quite pin down. Girls had always been a mystery to him, leaving him unsure and socially awkward. He often puzzled over his feelings, wondering what part of him wanted what. But he reminded himself that Zoe wasn't like other girls—she was simply a traveling companion. Yet still, he couldn't sort out what it was he felt.

Zoe interrupted his thoughts. "That ride back was something else," her voice more a playful question. "Just saying."

"Huh? Sorry, what did you say?"

Chapter 7

Ride to the Heart

Zoe slung the guitar over her shoulder and they continued their journey. Beside her, Arlo clutched Smitty's 'map' as they plunged through the now-familiar portal, determined to find the elusive path to the heart.

The swirl of colors and shapes from their first journey quickly gave way to a chaotic cell jam as their surroundings unraveled into pandemonium.

Arlo stepped forward with resolve. "What's happening here?" he asked a nearby cell. Zoe watched, ready to face whatever came their way.

The cell sighed, "There's a cholesterol blockage ahead. It's frustrating—when our host doesn't do their part, it's hard for me to do mine. Where're you off to?"

"The heart," Arlo replied, his voice steady with resolve.

The cell pointed to a narrow passage marked *Intake*. "You can squeeze through there. After that, you're on your own. But be quick—I feel storm clouds brewing."

After countless twists, turns, dead ends, and detours, Arlo and Zoe finally found themselves at the base of the heart, their mouths agape. It was a sight to behold, a moment when their struggles vanished and time stood still.

Zoe's voice softened, unable to fully capture the wonder before her. "Beautifully simple and elegant."

They spotted a nearby map stand with a bold red dot labeled *You Are Here*. Zoe deadpanned, "No kidding." Beside it, a stern *No Entry* sign blocked the way, while a contradictory *This Way to Reception* pointed straight ahead. They shrugged and set off down the path.

A woman in uniform stepped into their path, her voice sharp with disapproval. "And where do you think you're going?"

Arlo kept his cool. "Just looking around."

"Kids," she muttered. Her walkie-talkie crackled to life with a muffled voice. "Crapola," she grumbled, "I've got to go!"

Looking up, she pointed toward the reception. "Go. And don't touch anything."

Arlo and Zoe made their way to reception. The receptionist, seated behind a desk with a gleaming nameplate that read Cora, looked up and raised an eyebrow at the unexpected young visitors.

"Can we see Mr. Wattles?" Arlo asked, his voice shaky yet hopeful.

Cora masked her annoyance with a practiced smile, "I'm afraid he's busy and can't see guests now."

"But this is urgent," Arlo insisted, handing her Mr. Hershel's note. "This is a message for him."

Cora gestured dismissively toward a large tray brimming with notes, envelopes, and who knows what. "You'll have to leave it there."

Zoe glanced at the tray, her mind screaming, *Don't put it there.*

They hesitated, unsure of what to do, until Cora offered an alternative. "Our waiting area is full, but you can wait outside if you like."

"Okay, thanks," Zoe muttered, mustering more politeness than she felt was due.

They shuffled outside, heads low in quiet disappointment. Zoe, always quick to find a silver lining, gave Arlo a playful smile. "See that car in the VIP area? The one with the *Wattle* plate? I wonder whose car that is? How about we hang there while I strum some tunes?"

He chuckled, "I like the way you think."

Evening shadows crept over the parking lot. Cars vanished one by one, leaving Mr. Wattles' car as the sole survivor. Zoe was leaning against the bumper, practicing a melody she recently composed.

"You think he's got another car, or maybe. . .?" Arlo's question trailed off as the crunch of footsteps approached.

A deep voice cut through Zoe's melody. "Could you two please move?"

Arlo turned. "Mr. Wattles?"

With a wry smile, he replied, "The one and only."

"Mr. Hershel asked me to give you this," Arlo said, handing over the note with the urgency of a runner passing a relay baton.

As Mr. Wattles read the note, his annoyance melted into a warm chuckle. "Ah, Fred Hershel... Best of friends. Gem of a man. Sad to see him retire." Barely a heartbeat later, he added, "We don't usually offer tours. Sensitive area. Heart of the system. But if you're good with Fred, come back tomorrow. Cora will show you around." He leaned in with a soft glint in his eyes. "Cora's the sweetest person, but she can be a mother bear sometimes."

"We noticed," Zoe said. "Thanks."

"Gotta dash. Appointment waiting. Pleasure meeting you."

With a tip of his hat and a huge smile, he slid into his car and hurried off, leaving Arlo and Zoe in a quiet moment. The air around them hummed with the promise of another adventure.

* * *

Arlo and Zoe made their way to Cora's desk the next day. She glanced up, her expression softening into a smile. "Hey there. Sorry about yesterday. Mr. Wattles cleared things up. We all miss Fred around here."

She paused and smoothly shifted into professional mode. "Ready for a tour?" Without waiting for a response, she opened a drawer and handed out three masks. "Even the top-level inspectors wear these. You're about to enter one of our host's most vital organs—what we call The Pump."

As they followed Cora, the sound of rhythmic burps filled the air. Undeterred, she gestured to their surroundings, explaining each helper's crucial role.

Arlo glanced around, trying to pinpoint the source of the strange rhythm. "What's with the shaking?" he asked.

"Oh, you'll get used to it." Cora chuckled. "Look there. That's a sinus node, tirelessly pulsing electrical beats about every second. It's like a conductor that orchestrates the heart in circulating oxygen-rich blood. Fred managed that department. Few helpers are needed here since the heart relies heavily on the digestive system for support."

Arlo interjected proudly, "My dad's part of that team."

"Good to hear," Cora smiled. "We call them heroes up here. It takes a lot of human-helpers working together to keep the host's system running smoothly. These helpers, including your dad, have their work cut out with this host."

Arlo and Zoe occasionally bumped shoulders as they walked, their eyes meeting with wonder. Pretty cool, huh? Their glances seemed to say.

"I can't help wondering who our host thinks he is," Cora mused. "Why wouldn't he take better care of his most precious instrument?" She sighed. "No backup? Really? If this pump malfunctions and we can't get it back online quickly, it's lights out. That's a lot of motivation for us, including your dad. Our host is likely unaware of how much he relies on all of us. Without us, there's no host. But it's a two-way street—his survival hinges on us as much as ours on him."

As they continued, the heart's inner chamber opened, grand and glowing, leaving Arlo, Zoe, and even Cora momentarily speechless. Arlo and Zoe exchanged excited glances, an unspoken bond growing with each shared smile. Cora's voice faded as ethereal music seeped from the walls. Could something more be blooming in this life-giving space? Love, perhaps?

Chapter 8

The Heart Café

Mira closed the book and let it fall with a soft thud onto the coffee table. "How about a quick stroll around the neighborhood? Some leg stretching before the next chapter?"

Alexi shrugged. "Whatever."

Outside, the wet pavement reflected the sun's rays as it peeked through the clouds. Mira took a deep breath, savoring the fresh, earthy scent. "Are you liking the book?"

Alexi kicked a pebble. "Yeah, I guess. But it's not as good as *Harry Potter*."

"You think?" Mira chuckled. "I don't see this one landing on the bestseller list. It breaks a lot of storybook rules."

Alexi perked up. Her English teacher had been tutoring her in creative writing. "Really? Like what?"

"After you were born, I took a three-year leave from the hospital. When I wasn't changing diapers, I studied writing techniques and tried writing a book about life with your grandmother."

"But what rules does it break?"

"I think the biggest one is the 'show, don't tell' thing." Mira began. "Also, Arlo and Zoe don't face enough conflict. There's no big villain or huge stakes. I think these are overemphasized nowadays, but editors and teens expect fast-moving action. But what do I know? I never managed to get my book off the ground. Turns out, writing is a lot harder than critiquing."

They meandered through the deserted streets, chatting about their favorite parts.

"I have a question for you. Which character do you identify with?" Mira asked.

"Zoe, for sure."

"Really? Why Zoe?"

"Because I want to be like her when I get to High School."

Mira tilted her head. "I'd say you're a dead ringer for Arlo. But let's finish the book, and we can talk about it later if you like."

Once home, Alexi headed to the kitchen to pour herself a glass of juice, its deep purple glowing in the sunlight streaming through the window. They settled back onto the couch, and Mira picked up the thread of the story.

* * *

After the tour, Cora directed Arlo and Zoe to *The Heart Café*. They weaved through the café and found a small table in the corner. Arlo slid his chair closer to Zoe with a subtle yet intentional move. As they chit-chatted, she became increasingly pensive. "My mom used to say things like that to me."

"Things like what?"

"You know, what Cora said during the tour," she continued, "Who does Eric think he is? When my mom would ask me, 'Who do you think you are?' I knew something was up between us. Then, I would think, *yeah, who do I think I am?* I would ask: *Am I smart? Am I pretty?* None of those answers felt like the real me. One day, walking to school, it hit me.

I realized that everything I thought about myself wasn't the real me. If I were what my thoughts told me, I'd be a confused mess."

"As opposed to...?" Arlo teased.

She nudged his shoulder. "Ever since, I've wondered who I really am."

"You're starting to sound like Mr. Hershel. Do you think about this stuff a lot?"

"Not much. But I feel there's more to me than just a white blood cell. My last home before this host felt more inspiring. Karen told me there are guardians in some neighborhoods who know stuff like that."

Arlo scrunched his forehead, puzzled. "Guard ants? Do you think Eric has any?"

Zoe stifled a giggle. "Guardians—they're guardians. I don't know if Eric has any, but…"

Her voice trailed off, and Arlo jumped in. "But looking for them sounds like fun. I'm in."

Zoe's face lit up. "You mean that?"

"Absolutely. Guardianville, here we come."

They left the café and hopped into the first capsule they spotted. It propelled them out of the heart and onto their next adventure.

* * *

Zoe peered into the maze of branching arteries, uncertain where to exit. Shrugging, she pointed, "How about this one?"

They stepped from the capsule into a grim neighborhood where shadows clung to every corner and viruses prowled like predators, waiting to strike. A thick, tangible sense of danger permeated the air. Arlo scanned the dark streets, his voice dropping to a cautious whisper. "Know where we are?"

"Yeah," she whispered with a shudder. "Someplace scary."

Arlo caught a faint gleam of light in the distance. "There—let's go." They moved quickly. The sense of being hunted slowly faded as shadows gave way to a brighter area. They paused, feeling a sense of relief as they both exhaled.

Zoe shivered one last time before steadying herself, her voice firm with resolve. "Alright, let's go find a Guardian."

Their inquiries were met with shrugs. A guy in a T-shirt with Ignorance vs. Apathy printed on it waved them off. "Nah, don't know and don't care." Zoe chuckled, the absurdity lightening the mood.

Yet the hunt dragged on. Their pace slowed, shoulders sagging as they exchanged weary glances. As they wandered aimlessly, accepting defeat, a face they recognized walked toward them. "Hi, Greg here. We talked earlier. I got to thinking if you might be looking for Captain Weird?"

Arlo and Zoe shared puzzled looks, but Greg didn't pause. "People call him that now. Used to be normal, but these days, seems to have his head in the clouds. If anyone knows about Guardians, it's him. He works at the *Outer Spheres Bookstore* down the street. Name's Boggs. He always wears a T-shirt with the word *Nowhere* written on it. Good Luck."

Chapter 9

Boggs Offers Help

Arlo and Zoe entered the bookstore, mesmerized by the unfamiliar sights. Books, pictures, and curious items filled every nook and cranny, and did indeed look like objects from the outer spheres. They drifted through the shop, caught in the spell of its strange, magical ambiance.

Eventually, Arlo approached the counter. "Excuse me, do you know a fellow named Boggs?"

The clerk barely glanced up, raising an eyebrow with apparent disdain. "Oh, him. He comes in at six o'clock."

"That's an hour from now. Mind if we look around till then?"

With a lazy 'whatever' wave, she turned away, yawning like the world owed her more than this job. Arlo and Zoe wandered back into the maze of shelves, losing themselves among the books, crystal balls, bells, and incense—each discovery more intriguing than the last.

Time slipped away until Arlo felt a tap on his shoulder. "Tina said you were looking for me," the man said, gesturing toward the clerk, who was already rushing out the door. "Name's Boggs. Need help finding something?"

"We aren't exactly sure," Arlo admitted.

Boggs pointed to the word Nowhere emblazoned on his shirt. "Perfect. If you don't know, you're in the right place."

"Are you serious?" Arlo asked.

"Gee, no one's ever accused me of that before," Boggs chuckled.

"We're on an adventure," Zoe chimed in, "and looking for a guardian. Like someone who could help us see things… differently. Do you have any of them around here?"

"Duh squared," Boggs laughed as he waved his hand around the room. He pulled a few books off the shelves and read the titles aloud: *Enzyme Delirium*, *When Good White Blood Cells Go Bad*, and *Human-Helpers Who Need Help*. "No shortage of eye-openers here. I go to this meeting where we talk about stuff like that."

He walked to a display table and picked up a book titled *Where Are You Going in Such a Hurry?* "Kay, our group facilitator, wrote it. We meet every Friday night. Hmm, that's tomorrow. Gonna be around?"

Arlo shrugged, "*Nah*," blending with Zoe's "*Definitely*."

"You guys must be married," Boggs quipped as Arlo and Zoe exchanged uneasy glances. "All seriousness aside, it's more awesome than sightseeing. Oh hell, just come."

"I think it could be fun and a chance to chill," Zoe suggested.

"We'll meet here tomorrow night at 10," Boggs announced, leaving no room for discussion. "You'll like her. She's totally freeze."

* * *

The next evening, the trio headed to the meeting. "Looks

like our host has indigestion again," Boggs explained as a tremor rippled beneath their feet.

"We get it. The same thing happens in our neighborhood," Zoe responded.

"I like showing up early for some socializing before we get down to business," Boggs clowned as he rolled up his T-shirt sleeves. After walking a few blocks, he pointed to a sign neatly placed above a building: *Where Are You Going?*

"We're going there? Ugh." Arlo's voice rose in disbelief.

Inside, Arlo and Zoe exchanged wide-eyed glances, taking in the diverse mix of cellular organisms—chatting, snacking, drinking, hanging out. After a few introductions, Boggs excused himself to rendezvous with his girlfriend.

Arlo and Zoe were captivated as they explored the room, taking in all the vibrant images and colors, a visual feast that reminded them of the bookstore. Zoe spotted a poster and read aloud, *It's better to break a bone than a heart. You've got plenty of bones to spare.* Arlo chuckled and then pointed out another poster, bathed in dreamy purples and indigo, adorned with whimsical flowers and an intriguing phrase: *Wherever you go, you are always here.* He shrugged and then pointed out a cartoon pinned to the wall: *If you live in the present, you may not be opened until Christmas.*

"Welcome, folks," Marsha interrupted, breaking their focus from the wall of wisdom. "Boggs tells me you're new here."

Arlo nodded. "Yeah, we're passing through. Can you tell us what goes on here?"

"Honestly? No clue," Marsha admitted. "If I knew, there'd be no reason to be here every Friday. You two an item?"

"Just friends," Arlo responded quickly, almost too quickly.

"Oh yeah, I see," Marsha nodded.

After some light conversation, Zoe asked Marsha where she was from.

"I work in the head division—Central Control of the Command Center. We cover everything from C to C." Marsha paused, waiting for a laugh that didn't land. "Inside joke, I guess," she muttered.

Before Marsha could continue, she was interrupted by a bell. Some of the group sat on the floor while others chose chairs in the back of the room. Marsha noticed Arlo struggling to sit comfortably and fetched him a floor cushion.

Chapter 10

Revelations Afoot

"Welcome, folks! As always, it's a pleasure to be with you." Kay's casual smile, unassuming jeans, and no-frills blouse caught Arlo and Zoe by surprise. They exchanged a glance, barely holding back their chuckles. Marsha leaned in and whispered, "Not what you expected to see, huh? She usually begins with a joke—gets everyone here on time."

Kay's voice filled the room. "Most of you have heard stories about my bigwig brother-in-law Jacob, right? He's the VP at his company, and now he's itching to replace the President, who's retiring. The decision is Friday at 2 PM sharp. Jacob leaves early, but bam! Traffic's a nightmare. He arrives with ten minutes to spare but can't find any parking. After three laps around the block, he gets religious: 'Listen, God, I know I'm not your MVP, but if you help me with one small parking spot, I'll donate 10% of my salary to charity and swear off swearing. Please, God. Please.'"

Kay's face lit up, "And miracle of miracles, with one minute to spare, he rounds the corner, and a car pulls out right in front of the building. Jacob zips in, slams the brakes, and looks up: 'Never mind God, I found one.'"

The room filled with laughter, and after a few initial remarks, she began. "I'm not here to teach or preach. We're here to discuss one thing—*where are you going?* But first, I see we have a couple of newbies here tonight. What brought you here?"

Zoe took the lead. "We're on an adventure. We felt a little cramped at home," Zoe said, glancing at Arlo. "True?"

Arlo looked at Kay with a nod, "Yeah. I mean, yes, ma'am."

She waved off the formality. "Oh, we don't do any of that ma'am stuff around here. That's a big problem with most folks—wanting to be special. Being special is no fun. It makes you feel above others, and that's a lonely place."

Arlo's nerves eased a little. "Why do you call this place *Where are You Going?*"

Kay smiled. "Most folks aren't happy with who they are and where they're heading. They're constantly running toward the next promise of happiness. In our conversations, we explore the essence of who you are. Only then will you understand where you're going."

"But I don't want to be who I am," he frowned. "I want to do great things. My dad is ordinary, and..." his gaze dropped.

Kay gently interrupted, "Is he happy?"

Arlo blushed, "Well… yeah, I guess."

Kay's calm presence filled the room. "I have no issues with being the president of a company, but promotions only make you believe happiness depends on achieving the next rung on the ladder. Only when you're at peace with who you are, right here and right now, will you be truly happy."

"I don't get it." Arlo muttered, shifting uncomfortably, "Sometimes I feel so stupid."

Kay leaned forward. "I see. Sometimes you feel stupid…"

"Also, sometimes smart," Zoe cut in.

As Kay continued speaking, Zoe's posture straightened, a shiver running through her as long-unspoken truths snapped into place. If cells could have goosebumps, she'd be covered in them now.

"Okay," Kay pressed on, looking at Arlo. "You're a kaleidoscope of moods. Sometimes stupid and sometimes smart, sometimes angry, sometimes at ease, sad, happy, calm, fearful. Need I continue? I suggest you look beneath all that clutter and observe the part of yourself that is always peaceful and loving. That is who you truly are. Can you do that, Arlo?"

Arlo remained silent. Kay sensed his hesitation and continued, "I sense your girlfriend is already familiar with this."

"First of all," Arlo's frustration bubbling up, his voice louder than intended. "She's not my girlfriend, and second, she's smart."

Kay kept her tone light. "Well, you are friends, and she's a girl, so technically… But this has nothing to do with intelligence. The good news is that peace and love already exist within you."

When the meeting ended, Boggs walked over to Arlo and Zoe. "Cool, huh?"

"Not what I expected," Arlo said, his shoulders sagging. "I hoped I'd learn how to improve my life."

"Ah, but that's the problem," Boggs offered, trying his hand at Wisdom 101. "We're always looking for something better than what we have here."

Boggs paused as Kay walked up.

"How ya doing, Arlo?" she asked.

"I still don't get why you call this place *Where Are You Going?*"

Kay smiled. Think of it like your adventure. If you don't know where you're going, who knows where you may end up. Where are you going in life, Arlo?"

He shrugged. "I don't know. But for sure, somewhere different than where I am now."

"Ah, the elusive 'somewhere else,'" Kay mused. "On your travels, you must have seen maps with red dots with the words *You are Here*, right?" Arlo nodded.

"Where we are now is here, and 'here' is the only place you can ever be." Kay paused, letting the thought settle. "You can never be anywhere else because the moment you're 'there,' you'll see another red dot saying, *You are Here*."

"I never thought of it like that," Arlo reflected. "Wherever I go, I am always *here*. It's like the poster on your wall."

"Exactly. Merely drop the 't' from 'there.'" Kay caught the hint of a smile on his face. "I'm suggesting that wherever you are, you need to find comfort and peace inside here," Kay placed her hand on Arlo's heart, and he jolted in genuine shock. "The only way is to…"

"Yeah, I know—find out who I am," Arlo finished her sentence. "It seems like those words are haunting me. But how do I go about finding who I am?"

Kay's voice softened. "Finding who you are is the numero uno journey of a lifetime. Don't complicate it by searching for love and peace 'out there.' I suggest you love and accept what you have right here," she paused, glancing at Zoe. "That's a good first step. The love and happiness you seek are present here and now, quietly waiting for you to notice." Kay began to walk away. "Once you find the love inside, the outside will love you back."

As Arlo, Zoe, and Boggs left the building, Boggs asked Arlo what he thought of Kay.

"Wow, Kay seriously scrambled my brain. I never thought of things like that before."

"Same here at first," Boggs said, then shifted into a passable imitation of Kay's voice, "But what I'm suggesting is don't overthink it."

Outside, Boggs stretched his arms for a group hug. "I love you guys," he declared with genuine warmth. As he turned to head back inside, Zoe noticed the words *Now Here* on the back of his shirt.

Zoe spun Arlo around and pointed.

"I get it," Arlo chuckled. "*Nowhere is Now Here*. Sweet."

Their laughter was cut short as Marsha hurried over, waving a napkin with her address and a hastily drawn map scribbled on it. "If you're passing through, here's an invite to check out my place in the attic. I'd love to hear more about your adventures." Taking the napkin and thanking her, they flagged a cab and waved goodbye.

Chapter 11

Deeper into the Unknown

Alexi's eyes fluttered open. "Mom, why'd you stop reading?"

"I thought you drifted off. Want me to continue?" Mira asked softly.

"Yeah, I guess I zoned out. Do you know what Kay meant by 'find who you are'?"

"Sort of. This is heavy stuff for a kid's book. I believe she means we always have this love and peace deep inside, no matter what we think and feel about ourselves. We miss it because we look for it, in money, success, or sports."

"That's deep, Mom," Alexi said, with playful teasing.

Mira laughed. "Just channeling my hippie side. Let's make some hot chocolate before we continue."

Alexi brought a cup of hot chocolate to the couch, marshmallows bobbing like tiny buoys, and settled next to her mom. As Mira began to read, the atmosphere in the room transformed. Arlo and Zoe sprang to life, drawing Alexi back into the story.

* * *

Arlo nudged Zoe as they sat in the back of the cab. "Did Kay blow your mind, or is it just me?"

"Yep, I hear you," she laughed. "She threw me for a loop, too. During the meeting, something inside me flipped. And now I feel crazy happy—and totally giddy."

"Well... Where are you going?" barked the driver.

"No, not there. We're already there." Arlo answered, pointing to the building's *Where Are You Going* sign. He and Zoe burst into uncontrollable giggles.

Unamused, the driver tapped the meter, "Fine. Wanna play games? It's your dime ticking away."

Zoe turned to Arlo with over-the-top seriousness, "Where are we going?" Their attempt to stay composed crumbled like they'd been bitten by the laugh bug.

The driver shook his head. "Crazy kids."

"Our plans are a bit uncertain," Zoe confessed, regaining her composure. "Any sightseeing tips, sir?"

"Name's Sid, not sir," he corrected, nodding towards the license on his dash. This time, Arlo and Zoe managed to stifle their giggles.

"Oh, just start driving. We'll figure it out," Zoe said as she waved Sid forward. A moment later, she glanced at Arlo. "Maybe we should take Marsha up on her offer."

Sid turned around and glanced over his glasses. "Ya guys got credit on your card?"

"Yup," Arlo replied, then turned to Zoe. "My dad gave me his work card. Said it's got plenty of credit, and he and Mom wouldn't be using it anytime soon."

"Your dad seems pretty special." She winced, second-guessing her choice of words. "I mean, he seems sweet and caring. I wish I had a dad like that."

Arlo moved closer to Zoe, but not as close as he would have

liked. "Yeah," he sighed.

After a few seconds, Arlo leaned forward. "Can you take us to the head—you know, the Command Center?"

Sid shook his head. "No can do. Off-limits for us cabbies. One slip, and—it's curtains," he mimed tightening a noose around his neck. "But if you're serious, there's a station up ahead where I can drop you off."

Arlo nodded. When they arrived, Sid gestured toward the spinal column. Arlo and Zoe stared wide-eyed. The corridor shimmered with a web of glowing pathways.

"Us cabbies call it the *Expressway to Heaven*—straight shot to the Command Center. Best hop off here," he suggested, pointing to a nearby off-ramp. "But be careful."

"Be careful?" Arlo echoed.

Sid shrugged, "Heard there's some tough sledding getting there, and if you make it, ain't gonna be no picnic. Place's crawling with them snooty types. But hey, your funeral."

After a quick glance at each other, Arlo and Zoe gave Sid a thumbs-up. As they got out of the cab, Sid rolled down his window. "Ya know, you kids ain't so bad. Just don't let them smarties rub off on you, and don't make any mistakes."

"We'll try, sir," Arlo responded.

"Good start," Sid chuckled as he rolled up the window and drove off.

Chapter 12

Expressway to Heaven

Arlo and Zoe headed toward the towering ramp Sid described. It led them to an entrance framed by two massive discs, standing like guards from another world. Zoe tightened her guitar case to her back as she squeezed through the narrow passage.

Arlo's voice rang out behind her. "Wait. Did you see the sign over the entrance?"

Zoe glanced at Arlo, then at the backside of the foreboding *Enter at Your Own Risk* sign—but it was too late. It was during that moment of hesitation that the opening between the discs suddenly contracted. Her arm got caught in the vice-like grip, the guitar on her back strummed its final chord.

Arlo's heart raced as Zoe cried out in pain, fear knotting his stomach. He wanted to do something, anything, but felt powerless against those mighty jaws. Amidst the chaos, a First Responder rushed up, his 'FR' insignia offering a glimmer of hope. He immediately got on his radio to call for backup.

The FR stayed calm, even as he painted a rather grim picture. "Och, our lad's gone off to dreamland in that chair of his, letting his disks do a proper crunching," his voice carried a heavy dose of Irish DNA. "We should be getting the lass out before those disks settle down.

Arlo scrambled for a solution beyond his capabilities. "What if I jam my knapsack into this slot?"

The FR shook his head. "That won't be doin' the job. But I've got a wee trick up me sleeve. I'll give our host's nerve a wee nudge. That'll get them a shiftin'."

"But which way?" Arlo's voice trembled with fear.

"Aye, there's the rub. Left's our friend." He paused, his expression darkening. "Right... well, let's not be speakin' of that now."

"Do it now," Zoe hollered in desperation as Arlo nodded in anguished agreement.

"Let's be at it," the FR agreed, moving swiftly as a gale. "Grab yer, and when ye feel a wee tug, push with all ye might. I'll get things movin' before ye know it."

Arlo gripped Zoe tightly, his heart hammering in his chest. A deep roar echoed as the disks shuddered. With a surge of energy he didn't know he had, he pushed forward. Zoe's scream cut through the chaos. Entangled, they spun out of control. Then everything became eerily quiet.

Arlo blinked through the blur of tears, holding Zoe's still body. "Are you okay? Zoe? Please, please, be okay,"

He held her silent form, time stretching painfully. He pressed his cheek next to hers and felt a faint smile.

"Arlo?" she whispered.

Relief washed over him. "I thought I'd lost you," he breathed, his voice trembling.

"What did you say?" Her voice was a mere whimper.

Arlo held her gently, "I was so scared," he confessed, feeling her relax in his arms.

"Are you going to send me back home?"

"No way," he replied firmly. "We're a team. We need to get you patched up."

The FR, ever vigilant, walked them to the shuttle stop. "It'll be here soon enough. Three stops to the clinic." Before he left, Arlo's curiosity got the better of his worry, and he asked about the weird sounds surrounding them.

"Aye, 'tis a queer sort of place you've landed," the FR replied. "We be nestled in a long, narrow tube where sounds grow big as legends and whispers echo like fairies in the twilight. 'Tis hollow, indeed, but alive with a buzzin' that would put a hive to shame. An army of messengers zips up and down, they do, swift as the wind on the moors, turning our wee tube into a whirlwind of secrets."

The FR teetered on the brink of unveiling more wonders of this mysterious place, but a glance at Zoe's pain halted him. He smiled gently, extended his hand, and, with a hint of melancholy, said, "I'm Conor and proper delighted to lend a hand."

After their farewells and a half-hug from Zoe, they waited for the shuttle, hearts light and brimming with relief and gratitude, knowing their adventure could continue.

Chapter 13

Is this Heaven?

In the clinic's waiting room, Zoe turned to Arlo. "You were crying!"

Arlo offered a half-smile. "Yeah, I know. When I cried in the past, it was out of bitterness and self-pity. This time was different."

Her voice softened, "How so?"

He shrugged, searching for words that seemed just out of reach. "I don't know, but I've never felt this way before. Something happened when we were with Kay, when she put her hand on my heart." Needing more time to figure out what that something was, he shifted the focus to Zoe. "What about you? How're you doing?"

"I'm good—mostly." Zoe winced as she touched her arm. "But when I was in the jaws of death"—she snickered—" something incredible happened. I felt my life slipping away, like I was one breath from death. But instead of feeling small and insignificant, I felt... huge. Peaceful."

Arlo nodded, noticing the spark in her voice as she recalled the memory. "Go on."

"It made me realize I'm more than just this." She ran her good hand down her body. "I've felt that way before, but Kay brought it back to life."

"Did you ever tell anyone else about that?" He asked, recognizing that talking was helping her focus on something other than the pain.

"My mom," Zoe smirked, rolling her eyes. "She told me not to bring that topic up again, or she would take me to the doctor for pills. She said if others found out, they'd take me away. But where? She told me I don't want to know."

"Did she scare you?" he asked.

"Of course not," Zoe laughed, rolling her eyes again. "That's her go-to when she doesn't know something. Parents! Well, when we become parents..." She stopped, her cheeks flushing. She gestured between them awkwardly. "Not us—I mean, not you and me, just... you know, parents."

Before Arlo could respond, the nurse called her name. With a sigh of relief, Zoe stood and walked to the nurse's office, leaving Arlo to his thoughts.

A while later, Zoe returned, her arm snug in a cast. "Behold, the new you," Arlo grinned. "Wanna stick around here?"

"There's something about this place I love," she mused, glancing around, "But I'm a bit dizzy. How about we find an express and visit Marsha?"

Arlo nodded in agreement. As they left the clinic, Zoe spotted Dawn, the nurse who assisted her, sitting in the break area. She gave Dawn a grateful wave, then walked over to ask for directions to the Command Center.

Dawn looked up from her book, smiling warmly. "I could, sure—but I'm surprised you want to go now. Zoe, you've got a newly minted cast, and trust me, that's not a fashion statement. You told me you were hitting the road for adventure. I suggest you rest here for a few days. You're already at the most extraordinary of places."

"Really?" Arlo and Zoe replied in unison.

"No contest," Dawn assured them. "You've heard of the heart chakra, right?"

They shook their heads.

Dawn chuckled. "I'm amazed. Most cells search for this place and never find it, but you hit the jackpot without even buying a lottery ticket. Come inside and let me show you. I'm on break, and I enjoy sharing with others."

She led them to a small, empty room, just a wall chart, a lone table, and a few chairs. Dawn was in her element, poised to reveal the secrets of the universe.

Pointing to the chart with the flair of a seasoned lecturer, she began, "Chakras are a fancy name for energy centers that line up along the spinal column. All communication between the brain and body travels through this central channel, surrounded by spinal discs—an information superhighway, as I like to call it.

"For example, when I think about picking up my marker, my brain sends a message through this column, telling my hand to move. Without clear and constant communication between all branches of the body, the host is helpless. But that's only the tip of the iceberg."

Dawn smiled as if she was about to deliver a mind-blowing revelation. "On another level, this beautiful structure supports a stream of energy that flows from the spine's base to the crown of the head. This subtle energy is too fine to detect physically, so most hosts—doctors included—are clueless about its existence."

Wow! I find that amazing." Zoe interjected, encouraging her to continue.

"It's strange but true. And do you know where we are right now?"

Zoe shrugged as Dawn pointed to the chart. "We're here, smack-dab in the middle of the host's chest. If we journey down, three more energy chakras await, go up, and three more. These seven, highly trafficked hotspots along the spinal column serve as energy warehouses that influence the health and happiness of the host."

Zoe's eyes lit up. "No wonder the vibes here are unlike anything I've ever experienced."

"It's good you noticed," Dawn said with a smile, growing more animated and enjoying the exchanges. "Each chakra has its unique atmosphere, sort of like different countries."

"What country are we in now?" Arlo asked.

"This is Shangri-la," Dawn declared with panache. "This is the primo spot, just a heartbeat from the physical heart."

"We just came from there," Arlo added.

Dawn shook her head in amusement. "You two amaze me. It's not often outsiders mention being in the heart. I've been there myself, and as you've seen, it's a marvel. But here..." her words trailed off, and she gazed upward as if drawn to some unseen beauty. "This is the heart of the heart. I feel honored and blessed to work here. It's a continual emotional payday for me. Stick around. You'll see."

With a flourish, Dawn pointed to the top of the chart. "The dome, what you dubbed the Command Center, that's the real deal. It's more like a VIP spiritual lounge. The upper chakras, especially in the head, are vital for clarity and order. Without balance up there, chaos rules the body. You made a wise choice to head for the head," she laughed, clearly enjoying her theatrics, "but it's not the hug fest we've got here."

"Let's check this place out," Zoe blurted.

"Good call," Dawn said, handing them a miniaturized version of the chart. "Your arm will be fine, but chilling here is the best medicine. Before you jet to the stratosphere, check out why most visitors call this place the 'love-vibe' capital. I believe you'll find magic afoot." Dawn smiled mysteriously and winked, then walked them outside. "Start there," she said, pointing. "It's perfect for a couple like you." As they walked down the street, Arlo test-drove Dawn's words, *A couple like you*, and liked how that felt.

Chapter 14

Love Blossoms

Alexi put her hand on the book as Mira turned the page to begin a new chapter. "Mom, how about a pit stop?"

"Grand idea, that is," Mira said, testing her newfound Irish accent. "An' sure, I'm thinkin' our bellies are due for some food an a wee bit o' ice cream. What say ye, lass?" They shared a laugh.

After polishing off the leftover shrimp fried rice, they left the dishes in the sink and sat around the kitchen table. They laughed as they traded stories, attempting to outdo each other's best Irish impressions while scooping Rocky Road straight from the tub. So much of today felt like a joyful rebellion against Mira's usual kitchen routine.

When the conversation turned to Dawn's chakra presentation, Alexi asked, "Is it true doctors don't know about chakras?"

Mira nodded. "Yep. Modern medicine may not be so modern after all. Just because doctors can't see chakras doesn't mean they don't exist."

After a few more stories, Mira put the ice cream back in the freezer, and they settled back on the couch. Mira reached for the book, but Alexi stopped her. "I was thinking about that funny Bill Murray movie we watched last year—about those tiny heroes fighting germs inside his body."

Mira nodded. "I thought about that animated film, too. It's funny how easily I let go of my medical training the moment I saw those animated characters racing through his bloodstream in cars. But I like this book better. It pulls you in deeper and makes you see life differently—without the car chases. And the cool part? The author keeps it fun and relatable while keeping the biology part mostly spot-on. And honestly, who's to say we're any more 'real' than Arlo and Zoe?"

Alexi was silent, trying to take that in. Mira continued, "I had a chemistry professor who grabbed my attention. He told the class that the trillions of molecules in our bodies are 99.9% empty space. Everyone loved him because he had flair and would get us thinking outside the box. A few seconds before the end of class, he delivered the kicker: 'With all that space in us, how real are you?'"

Mira looked at Alexi, who seemed to have spaced out. She realized this was a difficult concept. After all, half her college class didn't get it. However, Mira let her words settle before picking up the book. "I think we're at the 'Dawn' of a new adventure," Alexi caught the cue and laughed, possibly more from the sugar high than the play on words.

* * *

Arlo and Zoe were strolling down the street, their attention drawn to a colorful building with a pink neon sign: *4th Street Chakra Club*. The hypnotic strumming of a guitar pulled them inside, where the air carried a subtle hint of rose and lavender. They settled at a table draped with a mint-green tablecloth.

They laughed, they chatted, the content of their words fading into the background. They became captivated, not by the food or ambiance, but by each other's presence. Time blurred. Their gazes met. An unspoken language flowed between them. The waiter glanced their way with envy in his eyes.

In a quiet moment, Zoe turned to Arlo, "I've been wondering what you were feeling when Eric's spinal disks went rogue on me."

His expression turned inward, reconnecting with the feeling he'd experienced mere hours before as a tear formed at the edge of his eye. "I was scared. It felt like one moment I had the most precious gift… then it was gone."

"A gift?"

"Maybe after we met Kay, I went off the deep end." Arlo admitted, his thoughts searching for the right words, "After we left her place, I… I felt something—something strong and unfamiliar. So, I don't know if it's real or not."

"Love?" Zoe asked, sliding her chair closer and wrapping her arm around him.

"Love. Yes." That word resonated in his chest in waves of bliss—or perhaps it was an arrow piercing his heart. Which? He didn't know. Yet, if there was any confusion, it was soon resolved when he looked at Zoe through watery eyes and, without a thought, leaned in and kissed her sweetly, innocently.

Zoe placed her hand on his chest "That's coming from here, yes?"

"Yes, the same place Kay touched."

This wasn't the clumsy kiss of a teen. It was tender and pure, born from a soul untouched by fiery passions. It was calm and peaceful, infused with a quiet energy that transcended experience.

His heart skipped a beat when Zoe placed her hand on his. The gentle pressure of their foreheads sent shivers down his spine. Their eyes met, and in that stillness, he realized they were no longer two travelers, but one, united by a profound connection. He felt that in every part of him, they were meant to be together, and he knew Zoe must feel it too, because it was the truth of this moment, and every moment to follow—a truth awakened by their first kiss.

But what was this feeling that was too wonderful, too new to express? His former idea of love now felt like a travesty. Yet there it was—*love*. Certain, yet mysterious, filling him with awe and gratitude. He instinctively knew that trying to capture this feeling in words would lessen its beauty, paradoxically, saying too much and too little.

He'd always believed love shouldn't hurt, but now he understood a deeper truth—an ache that breaks through the walls he'd built. It was a hurt that begged for more, drawing him closer to Zoe in ways he'd never imagined. He marveled at how their lives had intertwined in this quiet, perfect moment.

They sat hand in hand, wrapped in a silence that belonged only to them. Time bent. Minutes stretched into hours, as if the world had paused just for them. Their reverie was interrupted by the emcee asking if anyone had a song to share. Arlo nudged Zoe, but she shook her head and glanced at her arm.

Undeterred, Arlo sprang to his feet. "Yes, we have someone, but she lost her guitar in an accident. Can someone play for her?" The emcee beamed and signaled Zoe forward.

With a mix of shyness and excitement, she stepped onto the stage. Fumbling in her pocket, she pulled out a crumpled piece of paper. Her hands trembled as she handed it to the guitarist, explaining the chords. "I wrote this last night," Zoe explained, "so it's a bit rough."

The guitarist nodded and said, "Looks easy—simple chords." He strummed a few cords as he found the rhythm. Then, Zoe's voice joined in:

The world awakens and lights our space,
I gaze upon your handsome face.
Feelings so warm, having you near,
Our future together is crystal clear.
We belong together.

Our path ahead is bright, my dear,
Together we'll conquer our every fear.
The love we share is pure and true,
Forever and always, me and you.
We belong together.

As day unfolds in this land,
We walk together, hand in hand.
Birds sing from high above,
Nature seems to feel our love.
We belong together.

When evening comes, we stay up late,
The world outside will have to wait.
As we sleep, I hold you tight,
So much love we feel tonight.
We belong together.

When Zoe finished, the usual clinking of glasses and murmurs faded into an almost reverent hush. She stood rooted in place, feeling the spotlight grow hotter, the silence threatening to swallow her whole. Lowering her gaze, cheeks flushed, she stepped offstage. As the house lights brightened, applause erupted. She looked up in disbelief. Standing in a corner, their waiter wiped tears from his eyes.

Chapter 15

Joining Head and Heart

The following day, Arlo and Zoe were meandering aimlessly through quaint shops filled with heart-themed knick-knacks. Zoe was resting her head against Arlo's shoulder. "If I'm dreaming, let me sleep forever," she sighed.

"Ditto that," Arlo smiled. "But your song last night—you already knew, didn't you?"

"Oh, I've known for quite a while. So did Kay and Marsha."

"And Dawn?" He added to the list. "Sometimes I feel so clueless."

"Not clueless," she squeezed his hand. "Maybe a little slow on the uptake."

"Not only with you but with my family," Arlo admitted. "I've been thinking… maybe it's time to go home and see Mom and Dad."

Zoe's smile faded, realizing this might be the end of their adventure together. "Yes, your family..."

He searched her eyes, sensing her unspoken thoughts. "Dawn did say the fastest way out is up. Maybe we could swing by Marsha's place on the way. You still up for that?"

"Absolutely!" Her face lit up as she linked arms with him, a new energy in her stride.

* * *

Marsha's fingers raced across her keyboard in the Command Center, her eyes tracking every detail darting across her screens. When Arlo and Zoe strolled in, hands interlocked, she looked up, eyebrows arching. "Well now, welcome, explorers!" She giggled before noticing Zoe's arm. "Yikes!"

"Rookie mistake," Zoe waved it off with a dry smile.

Marsha leaped up and pulled them into a hug, "I'm thrilled you made it." She listened intently as they recounted their latest adventures, nodding and murmuring in all the right places. "It's perfect timing for a tour. Afterward, how about lunch?"

She tossed her jacket onto a chair and gestured to a panel of instruments. "I keep an eye on these gauges. If they turn red, we alert the specialists over there." She nodded toward a cluster of human-helpers in another section. "It's stress city when his brain gets activated, but our host is more sloth than cheetah, so the frontal cortex—my turf—mostly chill. Look over there and see where the real action happens."

Arlo and Zoe peered through the window, captivated by the frenetic network of firing synapses.

"Whoa," Arlo exhaled. "Makes Dad's job look like a cakewalk."

Marsha guided them through her workday maze, sharing insider tips—from the art of dodging long meetings to the tactics of avoiding office drama. As they looped back to her desk, she paused. "I couldn't help noticing you two holding hands. It seems you are substantially more of an item now than at Kay's. So, if you're considering, you know, becoming further itemized, there's a neat little chapel nearby."

Arlo shrugged, "Hmm," He said, looking at Zoe. "What do you think?"

"What do I think?" Zoe's voice came out sharper than intended.

Arlo stiffened, caught off guard by a possibility he hadn't considered before. He knew their bond went beyond ceremony. That first kiss sealed his promise. Before he could ruminate further, Marsha cut short his introspection. "Formally binding two cells is the most beautiful of unions. It's an unalterable contract that strengthens your commitment."

She beckoned Arlo to a side room and slipped off her ring. Stepping closer, she held it out to him, her voice dropping to a whisper, tinged with a hint of admonishment. "Arlo, you can do better than that. Do you remember how you felt when Kay touched your heart?"

Arlo nodded as Marsha gently placed the ring in his hand and said, "My husband died in the line of duty."

They walked back to Zoe, and without hesitation, he took her hand, closed his eyes for a moment, then said with quiet confidence, "I love holding your hand… but now I want to hold your heart too—forever."

Zoe blinked, unsure if she was hearing this.

Arlo took a deep breath. His voice was soft and steady. "Will you marry me?"

Zoe's face lit up. She leaped into Arlo's arms, forgetting her own.

"Ouchers!"

"Ouchers?" Marsha repeated, laughing. "I'll add that to my dictionary."

"Come, come," Marsha urged, "before our host wakes up from the couch and heads to bed," she snickered. "The chapel closes when our host becomes active. Zoe, come with me. I have something for you."

A few minutes later, they stepped into a warm, intimate chapel. A woman in an indigo dress stood by the altar, her amethyst pendant glinting softly—a striking contrast to the muted surroundings. Zoe was wearing Marsha's wedding dress, the lace wrapping her in delicate elegance.

Arlo fidgeted with the suit that once belonged to Marsha's husband. The sleeves dangled over his hands, and the trousers bunched at his ankles, but to Zoe, he looked magnificent.

"We keep it simple here," Pastor Shenley began. "Tell your partner you love them and wish to be one in love and peace."

With their hands clasped, Arlo and Zoe repeated the words softly, their voices blending effortlessly.

"Before we make it official, please share a few words. Zoe, would you like to start?"

"Happily," Zoe said, her eyes bright with excitement. "I made a list of six things I wanted to do for my New Year's Resolution. At the top was to travel with a friend. But life surprised me with a travel companion that I love."

Arlo paused, as his thoughts began to run amok, but he let go and let his words come from a place he'd only recently discovered. "Before you came into my life, I believed I could find happiness somewhere out there. But you showed me that happiness is found in my heart, and you are my heart. I love you as my partner, soulmate, and best friend."

The chapel walls seemed to glow as Pastor Shenley signed the certificate, and the newly minted couple sealed it with a kiss. Zoe winced from a twinge in her arm, and Arlo whispered, "Ouchers." Zoe giggled, swapping her signature playful shoulder thump for another kiss.

With the formalities now behind them, they settled into a relaxed lunch. Marsha leaned across the table. "Arlo, the grapevine's been buzzing. You want to get back to see your family. Right? But before you dash off, let me fill you in on some spectacular honeymoon spots."

* * *

Mira paused as Alexi let out a slow, contented breath. The tension in her shoulders softened, and for a moment, she seemed fragile and unguarded in a way Mira had never seen. It felt like Alexi had slipped into Zoe's shoes, in the middle of a teen romance novel. She turned toward Alexi, signaling that the author would now be speaking.

This marks the end of Arlo and Zoe's remarkable travels. I could go on and on about their many exciting adventures, ones that only the young can pull off—oh, when I was young—but let's save that for another day.

Arlo and Zoe continued to travel for almost a year (in human terms), and just as quickly as they'd decided to start their adventure, they knew it had come to an end. The thrill of the road had given way to something more profound, and both wanted to return home so Zoe could meet Arlo's parents. When they arrived, it was clear that their journey had brought them more than just memories—Zoe was carrying the beginnings of a new chapter in their lives.

Chapter 16
Love Prevails

Mira closed the book. "It's getting late. How about we call it a night?"

"I'm not tired," Alexi quickly responded. "Can we finish? Looks like it's the last chapter."

"Why not?" Mira said, riffling to the last chapter. "The author took some liberties again. White blood cells don't get pregnant. They are produced asexually in bone marrow and avoid all the drama."

"I did get an A in Biology, remember?"

"Yeah, I remember," Mira grinned. "As for the marriage thing? Seems a tad fast to me. But hey, I'm not a cell, so what do I know?"

Alexi scooted closer to Mira. She closed her eyes, picturing Arlo, now transformed into a knight in shining armor. And Zoe? Pretty much her twin, only more charming, cuter, and cooler.

* * *

Arlo and Zoe walked up the sidewalk to his house. He glanced at the overgrown yard. "Looks like Dad forgot to mow."

Zoe squeezed his hand, barely able to contain her excitement as Joyce burst from the house, wrapping Arlo in a long hug.

"I missed you, Mom," he said with a warm smile. "Or should I say Grandma?"

Joyce froze before his words settled in. Her eyes filled as she drew Zoe into a long hug, overwhelmed by a flood of emotion.

"Is Dad at work?" Arlo asked. "I can't wait to see his face when I tell him."

Joyce's smile faltered as a shadow crossed her face. "Arlo, your father..." Her voice quavered as she struggled for words.

Arlo opened his mouth to speak, but his throat was dry. Instead, he pulled her close.

"I wanted to see him so badly—to tell him that everything he'd been trying to tell me… I was such a fool."

Joyce shook her head. "Oh, no, your father would never have felt that way about you."

"But… but..."

"Let's go to the patio and talk," Joyce suggested. "Are you hungry? Thirsty?"

Joyce headed to the kitchen and returned with a tray of drinks and snacks, placing them on the table.

"Your dad talked about you with so much pride," Joyce said. "I, of course, thought he was a little crazy." Arlo chuckled weakly.

"Your dad loved me, loved life, and loved you, oh so much. He wasn't about money or status. Love and caring mattered to him, and he knew you also carried that gene. Sometimes he worried you weren't proud of him because of his job, but he was so much more than that. I was one of the few who knew that about him. He was a wonderful father and husband, and wanted you to be happy and share your gifts." She looked at Zoe, "Looks like mission accomplished."

With regret, Arlo thought about how he'd dismissed his father's wisdom. "He used to say, 'It's not what you do that matters; it's who you are inside.' Zoe helped me see that," Turning to his mom, he added, "I always thought Dad wanted me to be like him."

"Oh, no, he wanted you to be like you," Joyce spoke with quiet conviction. "He said that you were too overwhelmed with cell anxiety to realize how wonderful you are. We should all be so lucky to have a father like that. I have a letter for you. It's short because he was frail at the time. Read it aloud so Zoe can hear what your dad was like."

Arlo unfolded the letter and read:

> *Welcome home, Arlo. I hope your adventure was everything you hoped for. I wish I could have done that when I was your age, but taking care of my younger brothers got in the way. I know you wished I could have been different, but it's not what you do that matters; it's what you are inside. I tried to encourage you to choose a path with a heart. I hope I succeeded. I love you, Arlo. Dad.*

Arlo lowered his head as Zoe rubbed his back, and for a moment, no one said a word.

Joyce broke the silence, "So... where are you guys staying?"

"Well, ah... We haven't sorted that out yet," Arlo stammered while Zoe's shyness became more evident.

Joyce smiled. "Perfect. Then stay here. I could lend a hand with the new addition—and the lawn's not going to mow itself," she teased.

Arlo turned to Zoe. "Is that okay with you?"

Zoe's face lit up. She leaned in and kissed Joyce on the cheek, her smile saying it all.

Around them, the steady beat of the host's heart echoed faintly—a quiet reminder of where they'd been, and all that lay ahead.

* * *

Alexi was now snuggled up in a ball, nestled beside her mom. Mira slowly closed the book. They smiled at the animated images of the characters on the back cover, waving goodbye.

"You okay?" Mira asked, noticing a tear in Alexi's eye.

"Yeah, I liked it," Alexi murmured.

"Me too. Are you sad?"

"Kinda, but a happy sad. I remember when I was a kid. One night, you kissed me goodnight, turned off the lights, and closed my door, but the room didn't get dark. It became brighter than when the light was on, the brightest light I'd ever seen. It was weird, but I felt loved and cared for even more than you could ever love me. Crazy, huh? I didn't want to fall asleep, but I did. When you were reading about Arlo's love for Zoe, it felt a little like that."

"Maybe we should take you to see Dr. Burke for some pills?"

Alexi paused, then laughed, "Oh, Mom, you made a joke."

"But you never told me about that?"

"Yeah, I guess I forgot. You know—school, ballgames, and stuff." After sitting quietly for a minute, Alexi kissed her mom's cheek and said, "I love you, Mom," and with a smile, added, "Just saying."

"I love you too." Mira's heart swelled as she watched Alexi slowly walk up the steps to her room. A tear slipped down her cheek as she whispered, "I really, really love you, Alexi."

Part II:
Uncovering the Past

Chapter 17

Attic Treasures

"Alexi, the door," Mira warned, glancing up—but it was too late. The door slammed, rattling the pictures above her head as Alexi entered the living room.

Mira set her book down and peered at Alexi over her glasses. Despite the passage of years, the familiar worn wicker chairs and faded blue corduroy couch remained as they had been during Alexi's childhood. The bookcase shelves still sagged, weighed down by books heavier than their makers intended. The only noticeable change was the addition of framed photos of Alexi's college graduation and travels displayed on the wall.

"Sorry, Mom, but this is important," Alexi blurted out. "Where did you get that book you read to me when I was in eighth grade?"

Mira took off her glasses and looked up. "Book? What book are you talking about?"

"You know, the book about Arlo and Zoe, the white blood cells?" Alexi's words spilled out faster than intended—patience never her strong suit.

Mira frowned. "That's always been a bit of a mystery. It just showed up in our mailbox a few weeks before I read it to you.

No return address, nothing. I assumed it was from a book club that forgot to include promotional material. Why do you ask?"

"Do you remember who wrote it?" Alexi persisted.

"Oh, gosh! That was almost fifteen years ago. I hardly remember where I left my glasses fifteen minutes ago. But now that you mention it, the book didn't have an author's name, which I found odd. Who would write a book and omit their name? But I didn't think it was a big deal."

"But it is. Remember Lyam, the bicycle guy we went to when I was a kid?"

"I do. The week you turned seven, Dad and I got you a new bike, but the gears slipped. I took you to Lyam's bike shop down the street, and after that, you felt so grown-up, we let you go on your own. Don't you still go there when your bike needs attention?" Mira asked, wondering where this was heading.

"Yes! And I'd sometimes tell you stories about what Lyam and I talked about."

"And?"

"I'd tell you he sounded like that teacher, Kay, from the Arlo and Zoe book, but you'd just shrug."

"I also remember that Kay didn't like being called a teacher," Mira added.

"Anyway," Alexi cut to the chase, "yesterday, Lyam took me on his first balloon ride of the season."

"Nice. It must have been incredible—yesterday was Minnesota's warmest day of the year."

"More than the weather was incredible," Alexi said. "While we were inflating the balloon, a gust of wind yanked some of the stakes out of the ground. As Lyam held the balloon in place, he asked me to grab another support rope from the closet in his cabin. When I passed by his bedroom, the door was slightly open. I shouldn't have, but I took a quick peek inside. Above his desk was the same poster you have in your trunk, the same one

Arlo and Zoe saw at Kay's meeting. The *Wherever You Go, You Are There* poster."

"Interesting." Mira shook her head as she began to connect the dots. "I have a feeling where you're going with this."

"Just one more thing," Alexi concluded, tying up her case with a flair that would impress Sherlock Holmes. "I also noticed drawings of the characters from the book on his computer table. Of course, I might be a little crazy—Grandma Alice's genes and all—but seriously, do you think he wrote it? He says things that sound like the book."

"Such as?" Mira shifted position and placed her book on the coffee table, finding Alexi's story more engaging than the spy thriller she was reading.

"Well, once, during a balloon ride, he said, 'What we do in this life is as important as the hot air in this balloon.' Another time, on a bike ride, he compared our lives to the lives of cells."

"In the book, white blood cells are called human-helpers," Mira pointed out, mostly to herself than for Alexi.

"I know," Alexi smiled at the memory of that rainy day when her mom read her the book. "Can we go to the attic and look for that poster Grandma gave you?"

"Sure, but Alice didn't give it to me. It came with the suitcase."

"Suitcase?"

"Let's leave that tale for another day." Mira stood and swept her hand toward the staircase with a graceful bow. "Shall we?"

Mira glanced at Alexi as they reached the second floor. "You think your bicycle guy wrote the book?"

"No. Well—maybe," Alexi stammered. "I don't even know if he's *author* enough to write one, but he's full of zingers about life and why we're here."

The narrow staircase creaked as they climbed. Alexi pushed open the seldom-used attic door, and they stepped inside.

Drawings covered the bare drywall—a silent testament to forgotten creativity.

"Who do you think did all the artwork? "Mira teased with a playful wink.

"That was my Picasso phase," Alexi laughed. "But I was one up on him—my drawings have captions,"

"I like what you wrote here." Mira pointed to an abstract piece. '*If you try, it's not art.*'"

Alexi's voice softened, "I never get tired of coming up here. This one's my favorite." She pointed to a picture of herself sitting on a Pegasus, soaring against a star-speckled sky. "I love what you wrote under it: '*Now, ride as far as your dreams may take you.*'" The memory made Mira smile.

"In the corner, next to the chart Mira had drawn on the wall to track Alexi's height, sat an old rectangular trunk with a faded Peace Corps logo." Alexi stepped back as she lifted the trunk's lid. A waft of stale air escaped, as if it had been holding its breath for years and couldn't wait to exhale.

"I've always loved exploring the 'treasures' you brought back from the Peace Corps," Alexi said as she dug deeper into the trunk. "I especially like these... What are they called again?"

"Kulintangs. Traditional Filipino musicians have played them forever. I remember the kids in my neighborhood gathering to watch me play. I was good enough to perform at the school where I taught English. The rest is a time capsule of hippie artifacts that belong to Alice. As I may have mentioned, it was a wild ride back then."

"Yeah, about 500 times." Alexi rolled her eyes.

Engrossed in the trunk's contents, they forgot their purpose until Mira pulled out a creased and well-worn poster. Despite its tattered appearance, the psychedelic colors of the '60s remained vivid. She unfolded it and read, '*Wherever you go, You Are There.*'

"Wowzers, this is exactly like the poster in Lyam's cabin—

minus the rips and smudges. Kay also had a poster like that in her meeting room, but I never made the connection."

"Neither did I," Mira remarked. "Ah, here it is!" She pulled the book from a corner of the trunk. "I'm glad I saved it. I thought maybe if you ever..."

Alexi shot her a 'not this again' look, but unfazed, Mira continued flipping through the pages. "When I read that part, it struck me as a coincidence. Here we go. '*Wherever you go, you are always here.*' Hmm, slightly different from the actual posters."

"Yeah," Alexi nodded slowly." I do remember how cool it was. Wherever Arlo went, he was always here."

"My friends and I would try to 'be here now,'" Mira recalled. "But, as Kay pointed out, we are always already here, even before we try. It seemed too simple for us to believe." Mira started to place the book back into the trunk but hesitated, then handed it to Alexi. "Why don't you take it to Lyam and ask if he lost a book?"

"That's good, Mom. I'll do that. He's always so calm. Let's see if I can rock his boat."

As they wandered around the attic, opening boxes and revisiting their favorite keepsakes, Alexi found a song she had written in college.

Amid their rummaging, Mira casually suggested. "I'm going to see Alice next weekend. Care to join me? It's been a while since you last saw her."

"Yeah, I know. I never feel comfortable around her. It's like we barely speak the same language." Alexi picked up her mom's old guitar, hidden in a corner—a relic of rebellion, covered with peace signs and 'End the War' stickers.

"She never was warm and fuzzy, and she's become even more distant lately. It's not you, honey."

"Okay, I'm in," Alexi agreed. "I wonder if she knows anything about that poster. At least it'll give us something to talk about."

Mira nodded thoughtfully, "Maybe she does. However, remember that she's having trouble focusing lately. How about giving your song a go?"

Alexi smiled as she tuned the guitar. "It's called 'You're Already There.' It's been a while, so here goes nothing:"

The sun awakens from its sleep, ready for the fray.
Whatever comes, keep in mind your goal for this new day.
Keep the laughter flowing through the storm and the strife,
It's the essence of your journey; it's the melody of life.

Wave goodbye to your dreams; wake up to reality.
Surf the waves that haunt you, stop your worries, and be free.
No matter where you go, know you're already there,
Relax, let it happen, and love without a care.

Through the highs and the lows, enjoy the flow of life,
Dance and sing like children, bathe in eternal light.
Whatever you may ask, the where, the what, the how,
Recall that you are free in the beauty of the now.

When the road ahead seems endless, and your spirit's wearing thin,
Remember why you started, to feel the beauty that's within.
With every single heartbeat and every breath you take,
There's joy without an effort in every move you make.

With love as your compass and gratitude your guide,
Be mindful of your essence; keep your heart open wide.
Never forget to relish this amazing human form.
And thank the universe daily for the luck of being born.

Chapter 18

TGIF

As Alexi sat with her ninth-grade Biology students, she noticed a girl in the back. A wisp of auburn hair fell over her face as she stealthily checked her cell phone. Rita's mix of brightness and distraction brought back memories of her teenage struggles.

It was Friday, and the week's final class was slowly ticking away. Alexi's mind drifted to a cozy childhood memory: curled up on the sofa, listening to her mother read tales of Arlo and Zoe. This simple event sparked a lifelong curiosity, steering her toward becoming a biology teacher and a seeker of life's deeper truths.

"Rita," Alexi called out gently. Rita looked up, sheepishly placing her phone on her desk. Alexi channeled her eighth-grade teacher, Ms. Cheesman, miming picking up an invisible phone, turning it off, and tucking it into a backpack before beckoning Rita forward.

Rita's face flushed the color of her hair. She slipped her phone into her back pocket and walked to the front of the class.

Alexi looked at her, "These last few minutes are for starting your homework. I don't think your cell phone will help with this assignment. You can work with a couple of classmates if you like. Don't you want to join a group?" Rita shook her head.

"Well, I have something you might be interested in," Alexi continued, handing her a worksheet with a list of questions and a link to a video titled '*Inside the World of Our Bodies.*' "Watch this at home and answer the questions. It'll only take 20 minutes. If you do that, I'll toss out the test you took last week. Deal?"

Rita shrugged, muttering a barely audible, "Okay."

Alexi used this short, animated film with several of her students. It was a project she and Suki created in high school, inspired by ideas and characters from the Arlo and Zoe book. Since no copyright or author was listed, they assumed it was fair game. *Maybe soon I'll find out who the author is. Anyway, I'd like to discuss my upcoming bike race with Lyam.*

Alexi was lost in thought as the 3:30 p.m. final bell rang, and her students scrambled out, their day done. She was required to stay until 4 p.m. for hall duty or prep work, but her mind was already elsewhere, drifting toward thoughts of Lyam and wondering what Alice might know.

With her students' worksheets tucked in her briefcase, she pulled out the current issue of *Bicycle World.* She flipped through the pages, landing on the featured article about the notorious *Arrowhead 135*, Minnesota's grueling annual endurance race. The course started each January at International Falls, near the Canadian border, and spans 135 miles of snowy, treacherous terrain to the south.

Last year, an arctic chill of minus 55 degrees swept through the state, shutting down much of Minnesota and ending her race early, as it did for many others. She had faced tough challenges before, but the *Arrowhead 135* was on a whole new level of tough. Despite the bitter cold and pain, she was determined not to let it beat her and had already signed up for the following year's race. With a coach like Lyam, she thought 2020 would be different.

During her first year at the University of Minnesota, Alexi faced a hard truth: the middle school pitching star was now just another player warming the bench. With that, her Olympic gold medal dreams faded like a distant star. But Minneapolis, a haven for cyclists, offered new possibilities. One day, in her junior year, while at Lyam's shop, she overheard Matias—who went by Mati—chatting with Lyam. Mati's enthusiasm pulled her into an hour-long conversation. Before long, Minnesota's trails had become her second home, with Mati often riding beside her and off-road biking blossoming into her new passion.

Alexi initially scoffed when Mati first mentioned the *Arrowhead 135. Why would anyone want to freeze their bum on the coldest ride in the United States?* But Mati, with the gravity of a seasoned judge, took it to a new level as they rode together during Easter vacation.

"Even the Bible has a say on this race."

"You're messing with me, right?" Alexi replied, uncertain where this was heading.

"Not at all. The Bible clearly states that many are cold, but few are frozen."

Fighting a giggle, she told him, "Well, if the Bible's in on it, count me in next year."

Alexi sat at her desk, her mind divided. Teaching had brought her joy for the past four years, yet her resignation letter lay waiting in the drawer. She smiled, lost in thought. *I long to return to India, to the ashram life and peaceful meditations. I love India, but it often feels like it's playing the 'love me or leave me' game. And it's the perfect gateway to the rest of Asia. Now that Dad's Parkinson's is stabilized, Mom supports my adventures.*

Over the past few years, Alexi's life became intertwined with the weekly spiritual discussion group held at Steve's apartment, a tradition she discovered through a riding buddy. At first, she was reluctant—she didn't see the point in discussing something that, as Lyam would say, was "*unwordable*." But as the Fridays passed, many in the group began turning to her for advice and guidance. She hadn't shared much about her time in India or Lyam's wisdom, yet she was surprised by how easily the words flowed. She told her mom, "It's fun, and I enjoy it. If there's anything worth talking about, besides bikes, it's what Lyam calls the 'indescribable facts of life.'" The group grew quickly, soon filling Steve's living room and spilling into his kitchen and bedroom.

Alexi's thoughts drifted to Lyam. *I'm deeply grateful to him for supporting my races and the time we share. He feels more like a father to me than Dad. But did he write that book? And what about that poster on his wall—and those drawings of Arlo and Zoe? Next week, after hearing what Alice says, I'll have a showdown with him.*

As Alexi sank back into the comfort of her magazine, she heard a knock on her door and a familiar voice.

"Alexi, are you there?"

Oh, my God, I wish I were on hall duty. Gary is a great guy and teacher, but not my type.

Chapter 19
Uncovering Secrets

Mira guided her SUV down familiar country roads toward Alice's lakeside cabin. Alexi gazed out the window, watching the blur of green leaves. Her mind circled back to the mysterious poster woven into her family history.

The cabin's exterior—soaked from last night's rain—blended almost seamlessly with the surrounding cedar forest, save for the green tin roof. Alexi remembered when the cabin was a warm salmon hue back in the summers of her childhood, but time had weathered it into a darker, moodier shade that seemed to fit Alice as the two aged together.

On the deck, Alice sat wrapped in a blanket, staring out over the still water. A notebook rested on her lap beside a half-finished smoothie. Mira's voice was light as she greeted her mother.

Alice looked up with a small smile. "Yes, it is a lovely morning. But Alexi—what brings you here?"

"Hi, Alice," Alexi responded. Alice always wanted everyone to call her by her first name, never comfortable with Mom or Granny. "It's a beautiful day, and I've missed seeing you and the lake."

"I love the sun, and after the long winter—" Alice paused,

leaning forward in her chair. "Did you hear that? I love my loons. They're my steady companions. Now that the ice is melting, the male loons are back to stake out their territory. Their call always makes me happy."

Mira felt a vague sadness that Alice's favorite companions were solitary loons.

"But, Alexi, tell me—what's been happening in your life? How's the biking and teaching going?"

"Really?" Alexi blinked, surprised by Alice's sudden interest. "I'm glad you asked because last week something unusual happened, and I can't get it out of my head. Do you remember that poster Mom had in her room when she was living with you? The '*Wherever you go, you are there*' one?"

"Oh, we had so many posters," Alice leaned back, uncertain whether this conversation was heading toward a chapter she'd long since closed. "I don't remember that particular one."

"Well, I had never seen another one like it until yesterday," Alexi persisted. "That poster was also similar to one in a book Mom read to me when I was a kid. You know, the poster Mom took with her wherever she went?"

Alice remained straight-faced and silent.

"Do you remember me sometimes talking to you about the guy who repairs my bikes?"

Alice nodded, trying not to process what she felt may be coming next.

"Well, he took me for a balloon ride last weekend."

"That's nice."

"He's a far-out guy, about your age. Talks a lot about spiritual stuff, Native American traditions, Buddhism, and things he calls the facts of life."

Alice's jaw tightened as if bracing herself. "Hmm… the facts of life? What's his name?"

"Lyam."

"So, he's back," Alice muttered, her tone thick with disdain.

Mira's eyes widened at Alice's sudden change. It's as if Alexi had poked a sleeping bear. "What do you mean? Who's back?"

Alice fell silent, her brows drawing together as she stared over the water. She scoffed. "How should I know? Do I look like a mind reader?" Her sarcasm was so thick it was hard to tell if she was joking.

Mira and Alexi traded knowing glances—classic Alice dodging anything personal.

Alice abruptly shifted gears. "I'm tired. I need to rest. I know you like walking around the lake. I'll stay here."

Mira and Alexi set off on their walk. After a few minutes, Mira turned to Alexi. "There's something about this lake in spring. It's magical watching life wake up after a long, icy sleep."

"Totally." Alexi nodded, still caught up in thoughts of Alice and Lyam. "It's strange... Alice seemed willing to talk today, almost normal—until she wasn't."

Mira looked at Alexi as they walked the familiar path. "I know what you mean. Every time I visited her this year, it seemed like she wanted to communicate, to tell me something. Remember me telling you she's like a locked book? She's always been charming and competent and could cajole people into doing what she needed, and people liked her—but exposing her human side? That's another story. I never knew who she truly was or how we were with each other."

"That must have been hard for you," Alexi's words radiated heartfelt sympathy.

Their path intersected with a fallen tree brought down by an early spring ice storm. The sharp scent of cedar from its splintered trunk was hanging in the air. Mira walked around while Alexi saw it as a challenge and climbed over with an ease that spoke of her bold spirit—and age.

Reunited on the other side, Mira smiled. "Always up for

an adventure, huh?" Her thoughts then turned toward Alice. "You're right; it was hard at times. Once she shuts down, she's like a clam. Maybe you can come back next Sunday after you visit Lyam?"

Alexi's response was quick. "Let's do that, Mom. Do you want to come to Lyam's shop with me tomorrow?"

"No. Better you go alone."

Chapter 20

Connecting the Dots

Alexi locked her bike outside Lyam's shop. The bell above the door jingled as she stepped inside. With his usual effortless charm, Lyam was waving off a customer's attempt to find change.

"Keep it simple—an even twenty works."

When the customer left, Lyam turned toward Alexi with a big smile and asked about her bike.

"There's nothing wrong with my bike." Alexi's tone was firm, even edgy. "I have something important on my mind."

"Important, huh?" Lyam raised his eyebrows.

"Well, it's important to me—and my mom." Alexi cut to the chase. "That poster in your cabin. Where did you get it?"

"The one in my bedroom?"

"Yeah, I saw it last week when you asked me to get the rope for your balloon."

Lyam shifted uneasily, like a kid caught with his hand in the cookie jar.

"Why would you like to know?" But Alexi's 'the jig is up' look said it all. "Okay, I was wondering when you'd start putting the pieces together. That's why you were so quiet during our balloon ride, right?"

"Yeah. Shocked mostly. Things didn't add up, and I needed time to do the math."

"How about we walk down to the park?" Lyam suggested, nodding to Matt to keep an eye on the shop.

"Good idea. Sounds like you have a lot of saying to say."

Lyam's smile reappeared. "By the way, shouldn't you be teaching today?"

"I called in sick. I hardly slept last night after talking with Alice yesterday. You know who Alice is, right?"

Lyam hesitated before speaking. "Okay, here it is—I did know Alice. But many years ago, I promised to stay out of her and your mom's life. Over time, it became a promise that's been hard to keep. I kept my promise about Alice and your mom, but it didn't include you. I have no relatives or family, and I desired some connection."

"But why me? I don't get it. Why me?"

"I'm sorry, but that's a question for Alice, and I imagine that won't be an easy conversation. But if you want to know more about Alice and me, I can tell you where to go."

"I hope it's not where I'm thinking?" Alexi quipped.

Lyam chuckled. "To the place Mira was born."

"I know she was born on some reservation, but do you know which one?"

"I met Alice at the Hopi Reservation. We became friends there, and I spent time with your mother."

"Where was that?"

"Hotevilla. Hotevilla, Arizona." He repeated with a quiet reverence.

"I've never heard of that place. What's with all the mystery? And why won't Alice talk about the past?"

"Because she's a closed book."

"That helps," Alexi deadpanned. "I've heard that one before from Mom. This conversation is very frustrating."

"That's all I can say," Lyam's voice betrayed his frustration. "As long as Alice is still alive, I've agreed to keep her secrets, no matter how bizarre I find them."

"This isn't right and very unsettling. Why are you and Alice so secretive about Mom's past? And why did you send Mom that Arlo and Zoe book? I'm going back to see Alice."

* * *

Alexi and Mira drove to the cabin under dark clouds the following Sunday. Aside from a few brief texts, it was Alexi's first opportunity to tell her mom about her meeting with Lyam. After filling in the details, she added, "You'll like this, Mom. Before Lyam and I went for a walk, I pulled our mystery book out of my backpack, slid it across his counter, and asked if he'd lost a book. You should've seen the shock on his face. After a few seconds, he collected himself and calmly said, 'I wondered what happened to that book.'"

Mira chuckled, "Touché."

As the car hummed down the road, Alexi's thoughts drifted to Alice. "I hope Alice feels like talking today. I told Lyam I wasn't happy with our little interview. I think Alice has some major explaining to do."

"Good luck, honey. You got more out of her last week than I have in years."

They parked and followed the winding path to Alice's cabin just as a light drizzle began. Mira knocked on the unlocked door, then pushed it open. Alice was curled up on the couch under her favorite comforter, looking older than seventy-eight. She looked up, startled to see them.

"I told you I'd be back in a week to bring you fresh veggies," Mira reminded her.

"Yes, I remember. I'm just shocked to see Alexi so soon."

Dispensing with the usual small talk, Alexi dove in, "Alice. I've been thinking about our conversation last weekend, especially about Lyam." Alice was unmoved, although her face started to show signs of fatigue. "Neither Mom nor I have heard you mention Lyam before." Alice remained silent. "You never told anyone about him?"

"Of course not," Alice's face betrayed a hint of dry humor. "Do you think I'm crazy as a loon?"

She looked at Alexi and Mira. "You talked to Lya, huh?"

"Lya?" Alexi repeated.

Alice's voice became testy as she sat up. "Never mind—Lyam then,"

"Not us, only me," Alexi replied. "He said he promised to stay out of Mom's and your life. Is that right?"

"It's good he remembered," Alice exhaled slowly." But why are you talking to him? What did he tell you?"

"He keeps my bike tuned up, and I enjoy talking to him," Alexi continued. "He hasn't told me anything, if that's your concern. He said I should come to you for answers."

"Me?"

Mira noticed Alice's defenses rise, her shoulders stiffen, and her gaze turn inward. "Why can't you say something—anything—about your past, about my past?" she asked softly.

Alice's face displayed a mix of confusion and vulnerability for a moment—an expression Mira rarely saw. "I... I don't know," she murmured, her eyes closing in a heavy pause. "Let's leave the past where it belongs. I'm tired. I need to rest."

Unfazed, Alexi pressed on. "Lyam said he met you at the Hopi Reservation in Hotevilla, Arizona."

"Oh dear," Alice's voice barely reached a whisper. "I'm exhausted. I have to rest."

Alexi stood firm, waiting. After a long silence, Alice sighed. "Talk to Chief Dan."

* * *

After a quick walk around the lake, Alexi and Mira returned to the SUV for the drive home.

"I love her cabin, even on rainy days," Alexi mused, "but I wish it were more fun. Every time I leave, I feel drained."

Mira stared blankly at the road ahead.

"Mom, did you hear me?"

"Oh, what was that, honey?" Mira turned towards Alexi.

Alexi shook her head. "Nothing important. What were you thinking?"

"Just the usual suspects, Alice and Lyam. A walk around the lake always clears my head." Mira paused. "Do you realize the two of us have never taken a vacation together? How about a getaway this summer?"

Alexi caught the undertone, "Perhaps to a quaint town in Arizona?"

Mira laughed, "Too many knots need to be untangled. I feel like the belt on my pants needs to be loosened so I can breathe again. At any rate, your summer vacation begins next month."

"It's my last year teaching, so it will be a forever summer for me."

"It would be fun before you head back to India."

"Hmm, why not?" Alexi agreed. "I'll miss one small bike event with Mati, but let's do it. What about Dad and Alice?"

"They'll be fine without me for a couple of weeks," Mira reassured Alexi.

Chapter 21

The Road West

Mira's SUV, a relic from her softball mom days, sat in the driveway with its doors flung open like a bird ready for flight. Peeling and faded bumper stickers told stories of past adventures. Alexi and Mira buzzed around the car, cramming the last of their gear into every available nook for their "together trip" out west. Over the years, they'd become more than mother and daughter—they were best friends. For the next three weeks, they'd be trading fancy hotels—good luck finding any west of Minnesota—for something more rugged: a four-person tent Mira purchased for the trip.

Moreover, they each had five-inch-thick-down sleeping bags and a shareable queen-size inflatable air mattress. As for a plan? Explore as many national parks as possible before arriving in Hotevilla.

Mira glanced at Alexi before turning the car key. "Got everything?"

"Nope. I just don't know how far we'll get before I remember what I forgot."

Mira smiled as she pulled out of the driveway. "This reminds me of trips with Alice. Except with her, it was a lifestyle—and we stayed clear of my birthplace."

"How do you feel about going back?"

"A mix of nerves and excitement, especially after your chat with Lyam and his odd vow to steer clear of Alice and me. Makes you wonder, doesn't it?"

Alexi nodded. "We might be setting our hopes too high. Anyone who knew Alice or Lyam could be long gone. But still, I'm glad we're doing this. It'll be fun, and I'll make solid progress revamping Lyam's book. You think 'Who Am I?' still works as a title?"

"I was going to mention that. Lyam picked a good title. 'Who Am I?' gets to the core with three simple words."

Alexi shook her head in awe. "Amazing—my bike guy—a closet author."

Mira chuckled, "Did he ever tell you why he sent it to me?"

"He figured it'd help me get a grip on myself instead of moaning about everything and everyone—you included." Alexi turned toward Mira, catching a knowing grin. "He told me one evening he woke up and started writing, and four months later, it was finished. Before that, he'd never written anything, but when done, he felt certain it was meant for me."

"A true enigma, that man."

"Recently, I told him how his book helped me in my teens and suggested a revised version might help others. His response? *You're the writer—you should give it a shot.*" With the summer free and only a few bike races, it seemed like a good challenge."

"I wonder if he was sent to Earth to help wayward kids in a nontraditional way." Mira mused.

"Mom?"

"Sorry, I didn't mean it like that—though sometimes I struggled with your wild side."

Alexi grimaced as her mother's words hit home. "Once we get on a straightaway, I'd like to read you the chapter I just finished.

It's about how drugs affect the body and how human-helpers respond to them."

"Well, that sounds right up my alley."

"Did you ever do drugs—the recreational kind?"

Mira chuckled, "Sure, after all, it was the seventies."

"Do you regret it?"

"No, but I wasn't like Alice. I did very little, and they did expand my perspective on this little world I live in."

As they continued westward, endless fields of corn and soybeans marched past in precise, orderly rows. Here and there, barns and farmhouses broke the pattern, their reds and whites standing out against the earthy hues of the fields. The transition was seamless as they crossed into South Dakota, save for the golden wheat fields, now a patchwork of harvested stubble.

Now at the wheel, Alexi interrupted her mom's audiobook as they arrived in Aberdeen. "Are you as ready for lunch as I am? How about we find a picnic area with toilets?"

Mira nodded. "Sounds perfect. I hear those sandwiches and drinks in the cooler calling our names."

"What a pleasant drive so far. I'm glad we chose the path less traveled," Alexi mused while they settled into their first of many picnic areas. She unloaded the ice chest from the SUV and removed the contents while Mira pulled out their bag of meticulously packed utensils.

Mira's tone turned serious. "There's something I'm hesitant to tell you," She said as they sat at the picnic table.

Alexi looked up from her half-devoured egg salad sandwich. "Mom, that's a great way to start a topic."

Mira nodded. "You're right. Not good. When I saw Alice last week, I used her bathroom and saw an empty bottle of pain-killers in the wastebasket. I opened her medicine cabinet and saw two more bottles. On Wednesday, I called her doctor."

Alexi's eyes widened as she put down her sandwich, bracing

for what was to come. Mira took a deep breath and continued, "He told me Alice was diagnosed in July with an advanced brain tumor. She only has about six months to live unless she opts for surgery, which she declined."

Alexi swallowed hard. "Oh, my god. That's awful. But he told you those things?"

"Yes, perhaps he shouldn't have, but we have been friends from the first day I started working at the hospital. The medication might explain why she gets tired so quickly."

"I'm not sure how I feel about this," Alexi paused. "It makes me sad. Do you feel okay about this trip?"

"There's nothing to be done. I couldn't even tell Alice that I knew due to confidentiality. I'll check in with her every other day. We're cutting it close, but let's see how it goes. And we're only a long drive back if need be. She would never allow anyone to fuss over her anyway."

Chapter 22

Echoes of the Past

The sun stretched shadows across the South Dakota plains as it dipped low, a quiet farewell to the day. Alexi scrolled her cell for the nearest campsite, sighing with relief that they wouldn't end up in what Mira dubbed "stinky little hovels." Mira was chemically sensitive, and finding fragrance-free rooms would be nothing short of a 'Hail Mary.' They agreed that a campground in Bowman, North Dakota would be their home that evening.

Their first night under the stars, with "new everything," felt like a rite of passage. As the sky faded, they pitched their tent, and soon, the aroma of dinner filled the air. Alexi, chasing the last bits of pasta and veggies on her plate, broke into a contented smile.

"That was epic. Best meal I've ever had."

"Totally," Mira chuckled. "And our new stove works like a charm."

As night settled, the campfire crackled, casting a warm glow into the darkness. Their tent was dwarfed by RVs, some the size of a small country. They sat around the fire in foldable chairs, roasting marshmallows to a golden brown. In the quiet, Alexi grew thoughtful.

"Mom, you never told me much about Charlie and Ingrid. It's unlikely I'll hear anything about Alice's parents from her."

Mira sighed, "She's tight-lipped about her past. Seems like she'll carry her memories to the graveyard."

"And haunt that too!" Alexi's quip slipped out before she could catch herself. It was one of those times Alexi wished she could take back her words as the firelight caught the sadness in Mira's eyes. Mira had always felt a quiet ache over the disconnect between Alexi and Alice. She sensed now was the time to share Alice's childhood hardships.

"I tried talking about Alice's history, but you were about as interested as listening to an insurance agent."

"You're right, but I am now. Maybe I was too obsessed with myself to try to understand her," Alexi admitted.

Mira got up to put a pot of water on the stove as she reflected on how to begin. She settled back into her chair and, with a touch of theatrical flair, began to tell Alice's story. "The little I know about Alice is a tale of tragedy, a classic case of PTSD."

"Well, Mom, you certainly got my attention." Alexi straightened in her chair.

Mira smiled and continued. "Based on what Charlie told me on the few occasions we spoke, Alice had a tough time living with Ingrid. Alice never gave me any information about how to contact Charlie when I lived with her, but one day, I saw a letter she'd left on the table by mistake. It was from Charlie's lawyer about a trust fund he had set up for her. I was sixteen and brazen, so I called the lawyer. When I explained who I was, he told me to call back in a few days. When I called back, he gave me Charlie's number. After a few tries, I got through to him. We talked for a long time, and he answered all my questions."

"You only called him once?" Alexi voice spiked more than intended.

"Phone calls weren't cheap back then. When Alice got the

bill, she changed the phone number and added a code for long-distance calls. At any rate, Charlie told me he was a restaurateur and came to Minneapolis just before World War II to purchase a restaurant chain. While there, he became enchanted with rural Minnesota, learned to fish, bought some land, and built a cabin—the one Alice lives in now. On one of his trips, he met Ingrid, and they had Alice."

Mira's voice softened. "Charlie seemed to beam when he talked about his cabin and wanting to spend summers with Alice, but that wasn't to be. Ingrid had a drinking problem and was uncooperative. You could hear the pain in his voice, especially when he spoke about the accident."

"Accident?" Alexi blurted out.

"When Alice was eleven, Ingrid drove off a secluded country road, hit a tree, and died. Charlie's voice quivered when he told me how Alice, with a broken rib and concussion, was trapped in the wreckage beside her mother's lifeless body."

Alexi shuddered. "That explains the scar on her forehead."

Mira nodded, "It's hard to believe, but back then, seat belts were a thing of the future."

With a soft "whew," Alexi rose to add a log to the fire, nudging the outliers closer to the center. She busied herself with tea, trying to digest this revelation about Alice's tragic childhood. The aroma of peppermint filled her nostrils as she offered her mom a cup. Mira curled her fingers around the hot cup, took a thoughtful sip, and continued.

"Charlie wanted to take Alice, even before Ingrid's tragic end. He would have been a great father, but Ingrid wouldn't have it. Possibly, she couldn't face another failure. He did what he could, setting up a foundation to support Alice and eventually me. He was distant from his other children—he called them a bunch of entitled brats. But for us, he wanted to provide a better life."

"Charlie had other children?" Alexi asked rhetorically.

Mira nodded. "Three. When he found out about you, he also made sure the foundation funds were available for you. He invested wisely, growing the foundation's funds beyond our needs. He told me he failed as a family man in his early days but hoped to redeem himself. He probably thought, 'They've got to be better than the ones I have in New York.'"

A sense of awe softened Alexi's voice. "What an incredible story. What a remarkable man."

"Charlie died in 1998 when you were eight. He made everything official a few years earlier, but his kids still fought it—the greedy little bastards."

"Mom!" Alexi feigned shock, though a slight smile betrayed her amusement at Mira's uncharacteristic expletive.

"Sorry about that. I remember how hard your dad worked with a law professor at St. Cloud State to fight Charlie's kids. Your education, including your travels to India, was classified as educational and paid for by the foundation. Eventually, you'll need to contact the lawyer about the terms." Mira paused, considering. "Hmm, I wonder if it might cover your meetings if you decide to move out of Steve's living room. Let's look into that when we're home."

"So, India and school were paid for by Charlie," Alexi repeated with belated appreciation.

"I told you that when you went to college."

"I know, but I'm saying it now to reinforce my memory. I never knew the whole story. You also told me I could go to any college in the country. I guess I wasn't imaginative back then, picking the U of M, and not very interested in our family history. Maybe I also was an entitled brat."

"At times, you were," Mira conceded with a smile. "Anyway, maybe it's time to test our new tent."

They slipped into their sleeping bags, settling in for the night's expected 40-degree chill. The silence around them was filled with thoughts of their family's knotted past. After a few minutes, Alexi whispered, "Mom, who took care of Alice after the accident?"

Mira, teetering on the edge of sleep, murmured, "Good night, Alexi."

Chapter 23

Yellowstone Revelations

It was a crisp, clear morning, the temperature hovering in the low-fifties. Alexi and Mira were huddled around the camp's picnic table, savoring the aroma of cheese-topped omelets sizzling in the pan. Alexi set her steaming cup of hot chocolate on the table before flipping the fluffy omelets onto their plates. Mira spread cream cheese over the toast she had browned in a pan. As they ate, they marveled at how snug and warm their sleeping bags had felt during the night. Their laughter mingled with tales of Mira's nomadic teepee adventures with Alice.

After a whirlwind of cleaning and packing, they faced the puzzling reality that nothing fit in the car as it did when they left St. Cloud. Their gear seemed to have multiplied overnight and packing it back in delayed their departure.

"Finding my down vest in the van felt like a scavenger hunt," Alexi admitted. "We need to organize everything better tonight. But hey—Yellowstone, here we come."

Alexi glided the car along the winding country road, slicing through rolling prairies that stretched as far as the eye could see. Herds of cattle grazed here and there, oblivious to the passing travelers. After about fifteen minutes, Alexi looked towards Mira.

"I'm glad you told me about Charlie and Alice. It still gives me the chills to think about Alice in that wrecked car with Ingrid. Did anyone investigate?"

"It was rural Minnesota in the early fifties. Do you think anyone cared about the town drunk?"

"Ugh," Alexi uttered with a full-body shiver. "It wasn't a pleasant note to go to bed on. Sorry, I woke you, but do you know what happened to Alice after Ingrid died?"

Mira's tone warmed when she spoke of Charlie, a refreshing change from the audiobook she'd grown weary of. "At the funeral, Charlie asked Alice to return to New York with him, but Alice was seething with resentment. She blamed him for abandoning her—and for everything else her eleven-year-old mind could imagine. 'No' was the last word she ever spoke to him. After that, Ingrid's sister Anne stepped in as her guardian until Alice decided to take her defiance on the road, disappearing six years later."

"Hold on, how on earth did Charlie get wind of Ingrid's death?" Alexi probed.

"I asked him that. He said one of his restaurant managers in St. Cloud was his fishing buddy. I think Charlie knew more than we'll ever know. And I believe Jane told Charlie that Alice was going to San Francisco."

"Jane? Now that's a new piece on the chessboard."

Mira smiled, "Charlie once mentioned that Jane, Alice's friend, attended Ingrid's funeral. In his quiet way, Charlie would give her money to care for Ingrid's grave."

"I thought Alice went to the Hopi Reservation in Arizona?"

After all these years, Mira was thrilled to see Alexi's genuine interest in their history, particularly with Charlie, whose magic touch had made their lives so comfortable.

Leaving North Dakota behind, the green plains gave way to the rugged beauty of Big Sky Country. The road wound through small towns, frozen in time. Mira looked out at the landscape—*a perfect backdrop to revive the past.*

"Charlie thought the same," she said. "I'd love to hear that story from Alice because those two places are nowhere near each other. It seemed she was searching—for love, for acceptance, for some sense of normality—anything that might heal the wound she carried inside." Her voice softened. "I remember Charlie telling me that at Ingrid's funeral, he saw a wave of relief wash over Alice as the coffin was lowered into the ground. Perhaps she hoped her dark secrets would be buried along with her mother. She did keep them buried, but they live on, constantly resurfacing, haunting her life—and mine."

"And to some extent, mine," Alexi murmured, swirling with emotions. "Mom, I'm glad you're telling me this. You know how Alice rubs me the wrong way, and I never feel comfortable around her." She looked at Mira. "I'll try to see her differently now and practice the compassion we discuss at our meetings. I admire how you found your way after living with Alice all those years."

"Thanks," Mira replied. "As I mentioned, I had to work at it. But she didn't completely define me. My personality differs from hers, so I found my way. And Charlie—he was my hero. He set up a fund for Alice when she turned eighteen. He was considerate and stayed out of our lives because of Alice's insistence—no one wins with her. After he retired in '94, he called me. I was overjoyed to hear from him again. When I told him about you, he invited Dad, you, and me to visit him in New York. That Christmas with Charlie was magic. A vacation and a family reunion all in one."

Alexi stared ahead at the ribbon of asphalt that seemed to go nowhere forever. "I remember seeing the pictures of us standing with Charlie next to the Christmas tree at Rockefeller Center. I wish I had been old enough to remember him."

"Here's a tidbit you'll enjoy," Mira smiled. "In Charlie's den, I noticed a portrait of his mother, Alice Byron Armstrong. The quality was on par with the presidential portraits I've seen in the National Gallery. Alongside photos of her with the King of England was my favorite—little Charlie sitting on President Teddy Roosevelt's lap. I also recall a photo of him with his mother in Greece. On the bottom were the words, perhaps written by his mother: *Do good and be honorable, or life is a loss.*"

Alexi shivered. "This whole thing gives me goosebumps."

"Me too," Mira laughed softly. "I love talking about Charlie. He said the only thing besides money Ingrid would accept from him was a name for Alice. Despite being his mother's sole heir, his greatest inheritance was his generous heart. After our trip to New York, I would send him pictures of you. But enough, I'm rambling."

"Rambling's good. Keep going," Alexi encouraged.

"Enough chatter. Let's find some tunes." Mira reached for the radio and fiddled with the dial. Stations blurred by—classical, ads, Gospel, static. When a country station came through, she winked at Alexi, "When in Montana…"

Alexi giggled, grateful and feeling incredibly lucky to have a mom like this.

* * *

Mira and Alexi pulled into Mammoth Campground as the last rays of sunlight disappeared behind the mountains. Stepping out of the car, they were greeted by ravens putting on an aerial show. The air was rich with the scent of sagebrush after an afternoon shower, mingling with the sharp tang of sulfur. After setting up their tent, eating, and chillaxing, Alexi asked, "Are you up for some fun facts about Yellowstone?"

Mira nodded as she grabbed her down vest from the car.

"When we were at the Ranger Station, I found out that Yellowstone was the first national park—in the world. The foresight the early Americans had in doing that was amazing. I also thought it interesting that Yellowstone has more than half of all the geysers in the world, and right now, we're sitting on top of the largest potential super volcano in North America."

"A real hotspot," Mira quipped. "I wish it would heat the ground a little. My feet are starting to get cold."

Alexi smiled, "Want to take a walk before we turn in?"

After they returned, Alexi zipped up the tent, and they wriggled into their bags, sinking into the welcome relief of rest after a long day on the road. Gazing at the stars through the tent's netting, Alexi could make out the Milky Way. Beneath this vastness, she felt a profound connection to the infinite. She looked over to Mira, expecting an equally gob-smacked reaction. Instead, Mira was already lost in dreams, snoring gently. Alexi smiled and closed her eyes.

Chapter 24

Zion

Several days and a few parks later, Mira surveyed the warm glow of Zion's orange cliffs as the sun started to set. "Can you believe our luck?" Mira asked. "Another campsite snagged without a reservation. We're getting quite good at this. And I love that the showers are only a few minutes' walk away."

"Well, I have no reservations about staying here," Alexi said with a smirk. "I never worry about finding a spot. If the park is full, we camp outside the park and show up the next morning to nab one of the first-come, first-served sites. I don't know why more people don't think of that."

"Trusting in life is one trait we both inherited from Alice. It'll be dark soon, and we've only got time to set up the tent and grab a quick snack before I crash," Mira said, though she was sure Alexi would take a walk before turning in.

* * *

On their last day at Zion, Alexi and Mira walked to their campsite after a strenuous climb up the Mountain to Angels' Landing. Overhead, condors glided in slow, graceful loops against the clear blue sky. Crossing the bridge over the Virgin River, they shared a knowing smile—a quiet celebration of the previous day's trek up the river into that stunning slot canyon.

"Whew, what a day," Mira exhaled as she collapsed onto their picnic bench. "I'm beat, but a good beat. Two days is barely enough time for this park."

Alexi slipped off her headband and nodded. "Not enough time for any of these parks. It gives me chills thinking about everything we crammed into this trip. National parks might be one of the best things the US government does. It's an honor to have these places preserved for everyone."

They swapped their hiking boots for sneakers and headed for the showers. Later, as the sun crept behind the cliffs, Mira grabbed her vest and picked up the hiking map on the picnic table. She traced the route they had just taken with her finger before reluctantly folding it up.

She turned toward Alexi, "Our last adventure before Hotevilla!"

"By your tone, you'd think you were heading to your execution."

Mira laughed, "This trip has been magical, but I can't decide if I'm more excited or scared. Was I even born there? Enough—what's on the menu tonight?"

Alexi rummaged through the supply bag and looked up at Mira. "How about noodles and a packet of yummy Indian dahl with the last veggies before they go south? And for dessert, we still have—" She jumped back as a mouse scurried out. "Yikes! Guess I left the nuts out."

After dinner, they settled into their chairs, wine glasses in hand. Their minds wandered to the adventures of the past few weeks. Mira gleefully commented on her firmer body tone while Alexi's thoughts shifted from the bag of nuts they lost to Ms. Cheesman.

"I forgot to mention that Ms. Cheesman got married."

Mira's face lit up. "That's wonderful news. What a gem. I always loved chatting with her during our parent-teacher conferences."

"She went above and beyond the call of duty with me," Alexi grinned sheepishly. "I still feel bad about the dead mouse Ricky and I put in her desk drawer."

"What?" Mira's eyes widened.

"Bad, huh? You know, mouse, cheesy."

"Yeah, I get it, but I still think it stinks," Mira replied, hiding a smile.

Alexi blushed slightly. "Right before our trip, I saw her and apologized for all the pranks. She brushed it off with, 'We all have some sorry moments we wish came with a delete button.' I told her how her calmness was a lesson for me, and now when things get chaotic, I'd ask myself, 'What would Ms. Cheesman do?'"

"I thanked her and gave her a wedding gift with a poem I wrote. Without missing a beat, she said, 'I hope this isn't cheese.' She laughed and tapped my shoulder, saying, 'I knew there was something special about this one.' Then we shared a sweet hug."

They paused, smiling with amusement as they watched a young couple struggle with a tent fresh out of the box. They held fold-out instructions that reached the ground, most likely meant for a space station. Yet they persisted, doing and undoing poles in and out of grommets and slots.

As Alexi poured more wine, her expression shifted. "Mom, I have a confession to make."

Mira raised an eyebrow, "Oh?"

"After you read that Arlo and Zoe book to me, you know, in my out-of-control days, I went to my room and cried."

Mira was taken aback. "You did? But why?"

"A lot of reasons," Alexi murmured, tracing the rim of her

glass with a finger. "Like throwing a tantrum when our game got rained out. And for some of the mean things I did, even to the people I cared about, like you and Ms. Cheesman. I cried because I was afraid I'd never grow up and have a loving relationship like Arlo and Zoe. When we drove over that little chipmunk yesterday, I thought about that poor caterpillar I killed when I was a brat and how it would never turn into a beautiful butterfly."

Mira nodded slowly. "I get it. But you were just trying to figure things out."

After a pause, Mira readjusted her uneven chair and continued, "Caterpillars have always struck me as incredible creatures. They're like metaphors for our lives—crawling, then spreading their wings and taking flight. But working at the hospital, I'm constantly reminded that life and death are intertwined. In nature, something is always getting squashed or eaten. Each fish in the ocean is food for some other fish—or human. Someone once described our world as one vast, interconnected dining hall."

Alexi chuckled. "I like that. A grand buffet."

"The memory of that caterpillar you squashed makes me cringe," Mira said, "but what I remember most was your artistic endeavor on our living room wall."

"Oh, sorry about that one." Alexi chuckled as she remembered the incident. "You took me to the attic. I was scared you were going to lock me up there. But you handed me crayons and said, 'Use these walls.' I could be a little monster."

Alexi grabbed the tin of crackers from the supply bin. They watched with admiration their neighbors' victory dance around their upright tent. It was an architectural wonder that was equal parts skill and luck.

Mira raised her glass as she toasted their neighbor's triumph. "I also have a confession. That book was pivotal for me, too. After reading it to you, I saw a soft, vulnerable side you kept hidden behind teenage bravado. I realized it wasn't about you needing to grow up. It was about me. I was impatient, trying to shape you into my idea of who you should be. But you were the only thing you could be, a teenager, nothing more, nothing less."

Mira looked at Alexi, now twenty-nine, marveling at the strong friendship they'd built. "I wonder if Lyam had any idea how he changed our relationship. I hope we can learn more about him in the next few days.

Mira got up to pour the last of the wine. "Funny what a little Merlot reveals," she said, laughing as she sat back down and took in the incredible woman Alexi had become. "But enough. Wanna hear a joke?"

"Lay it on me," Alexi slurred, a little giddy from her third glass of wine.

Mira chuckled, also feeling the warmth from the wine. "This guy Ralph goes to a pet shop looking for something unique. The owner tells him it's his lucky day because he just got in an amazing talking caterpillar. 'His name's Levi, and he comes with his own jar and everything.' *Ya, sure,* Ralph thinks, but this is too tempting to pass on. He takes the plunge, and the next day asks Levi if he wants to go for a walk. Silence. An hour later, frustrated at himself for being such a doofus, he taps the jar and asks more sternly. Finally, a grumpy voice comes from inside the jar, 'Don't rush me already. I'm putting on my shoes.'"

Alexi's laughter carried beyond the confines of their site. They exchanged glances, setting off another round of giggles, this time more subdued. Mira leaned back in her chair. "Ah, today was fun. This has been one of my most wonderful trips—and I've been on quite a few."

"The night wore on, but neither brought up sleep. They sat under an almost full moon, talking in the gentle warmth of the evening."

With a mere five-hour drive to Hotevilla remaining, they planned on a quick detour to the Kanab Visitor Center. Alexi wasn't into souvenirs, but a poster of the slot canyon they walked through the day before—irresistible. Finally, the inevitable arrived—tent time. Mira reluctantly entered as Alexi took one last look at the cosmos, whispering a reverent "Namaste" before calling it a night.

Chapter 25

Hotevilla at Last

"Well, we're here—or are we?" Alexi said as they arrived in Hotevilla the following day. The town sat atop a mesa that overlooked the barren plains that stretched endlessly beneath the pale sky. A steady wind swept down the sandy streets lined with one-story brick and adobe homes—some showing signs of life, while others stood quiet and forgotten.

Mira surveyed the landscape, her mind grappling with the reality. "This isn't the Hopi village I pictured."

Alexi struggled to reconcile the vibrant stories of Mira's childhood with the scene in front of her. "I get what you mean… it's… well..."

"Depressing?" Mira cut in, sidestepping any euphemisms. "Maybe it looks this way because of the parks we've been to. Anyway, we're here, so let's see what we can make happen."

They approached a few people, asking where they might find the Hopi chief. They quickly learned that the chief was now referred to as the Chairman.

A young boy, idly kicking a soccer ball down the street, became their unintended guide. He led them to the Chairman, who informed them that Chief Dan had died many years ago.

"You need to find Doc if you want to know about the past. She's a shaman and might be able to help," he informed them in a brief and underwhelming conversation.

Mira and Alexi thanked him and left, disappointed that Chief Dan was no longer an option.

"Maybe this whole thing is a big mistake." Mira wondered aloud. "I'm not sure if this is even the right town. Now what?"

Alexi pointed out a small grocery store, about the size of a small cottage. The windows were barred, and outside stood a rusted gas pump that most likely hadn't seen action since dinosaur times. "Let's check it out and come up with a plan." The store was sparsely stocked, offering only the essentials except for an ice cream cooler.

They left the store and strolled along a deserted street, Dove ice cream bars in hand. "Let's try to find that doctor before we throw in the towel," Mira said, her spirits lifting with each bite.

As they meandered, a woman with a weathered face approached. "I hear you're looking for the Hopi chief. I'm sure that was productive," she chuckled softly. "As you probably now know, there are no more Hopi chiefs. They went out with twenty-cent gas. The Hopi tribe and Uncle Sam signed a charter sometime before World War II, swapping out chiefs for chairmen. Timothy, the man you met, is the current Chairman of the Hopi Reservation. Not very romantic, huh?"

Alexi and Mira exchanged amused glances, instantly charmed by her candor and commanding presence. "I'm Doc," she greeted them, "his sometimes cook."

"Great," Alexi replied. "The Chairman told us to find you. I'm Alexi, and this is my mom, Mira. She's also a doctor."

"I'm not a doctor," the woman laughed. "My name's Sofia. My Indian name means Daughter of the Clouds, so people call me Doc."

"Oh, yes, Daughter of the Clouds," Alexi smiled, feeling

at ease with her laid-back manner. "We came here to speak with Chief Dan. My grandmother knew him, and Chairman Timothy said you're the go-to person if we want to go that far back."

"Sure, let's sit on those rocks under that tree," Sofia suggested. "Let's see if I can help."

She led them to the dappled shade of a lone palo verde tree. Without hesitation, Alexi began. "My grandmother had a connection with the Hopi tribe and Chief Dan. We're trying to find out information about her and a fellow named Lyam."

"Lyam?" Sofia repeated, shocked by a name she hadn't heard in over twenty years.

Alexi became more animated. "You know him?"

"Know Lyam?" Sofia's face lit up. "We were as close as twins."

"What?" Alexi's voice rose. "I'm speechless."

"Wait a minute. Do you also know Alice?" Mira asked.

"Nooo," Sofia hesitated. "Well, maybe."

"Alice had connections with Lyam and Chief Dan," Mira said, sharing the only facts she knew.

Sofia searched her memory. "That was a long time ago. Chief Dan died in '72 when I was about thirty. I'd known him since I was a baby. Did Alice have a scar right here?" She touched her forehead.

"Yes," Mira nodded, "from a car accident when she was a child."

"Did she have a daughter who would be, hmm, simple math, about sixty? Wait, you—yes, I can tell it's you."

Mira stammered, "Me what?"

"Kaiya's and Cheveyo's daughter," Sofia's eyes met Mira's. "You're Alice and Lyam's daughter."

Mira fell silent, trying to process what she heard. In the back of her mind, a faint voice whispered that maybe, just maybe, she'd sensed this all along. Before her mind could fully engage,

Sofia continued. "Kaiya was the name Chief Dan gave her, which means Willow Tree—maybe because she was tall and slender."

Mira managed a shaky, "Let me get this straight. You're saying Lyam is my father?"

Sofia's voice softened, "I'm sorry… I see you didn't know. I assumed..." Her words trailed off as she saw tears welling up in Mira's eyes.

Mira let a few heartbeats pass before speaking. "That's alright. I'm not like others who need to know their parents. My mom was enough," she half-smiled. "I never imagined I would know my father, and now—what a world."

Alexi processed the revelation. "So, Lyam is my grandfather!"

The three grew quiet until Mira said, "I've asked Alice time and again who my father was, and she always said she didn't know."

"On the surface, it's not clear-cut. But I see there's a lot you don't know. I'm on my way to cook for the Chairman. We could continue tomorrow if you like. Do you have a place to stay?"

Alexi nodded, "Yes, in our tent."

"You can stay with my cousin," Sofia offered. "She has a spare room."

"That's kind of you," Alexi smiled appreciatively. "But we love our tent. Do you know where we could pitch it for the night?"

Sofia's gaze drifted to times gone by. "Tents! I sometimes wish we all lived in tents. It would make us more… Sorry, I sometimes get carried away." Sofia provided directions to a camping location and cautioned them about the limited food options in Hotevilla.

"No worries," Alexi replied. "Mom and I are self-sufficient. Besides, there's a lot more than food we'll be digesting tonight."

"Come to my place tomorrow morning," Sofia pointed down the street. "It's that little adobe structure that Cheveyo and I built."

Chapter 26

Sofia Weaves the Past

"Good morning," Sofia greeted them as they arrived. "I spoke with the Great Spirit last night and received a message to take you to my favorite power spot. Do you have hiking boots and a backpack?"

Alexi and Mira nodded, looking forward to this unexpected adventure.

"I packed lunch for us." Sofia continued. "Let's get your boots and water. It's a little over an hour's hike."

They set off along a less-than-obvious path that wound along the mesa. Unlike the dramatic crimson of Zion, the landscape here was a mix of pale whites and soft yellows, broken here and there by a juniper or shrub.

An hour later, they reached a small clearing tucked against a towering rock wall. Sofia performed a brief smudging ceremony—an indigenous ritual meant to purify and bless. The dry wind was constant, but the wall offered protection for the fragrant sage to waft around them. They each found a rock to sit on in the shade of the cliff.

"So, where to begin?" Sofia's voice broke through the quiet.

Alexi was first to ask, "You and Lyam are twins? I find that hard to wrap my head around."

Sofia's chuckle mingled with the sound of the wind. "In spirit only. Lyam's been with my family since he was a toddler."

"Well, that sounds like a good place to start," Mira chimed in, handing Sofia the reins as Alexi's questions took a back seat. "How did that happen?"

Sofia, the consummate teacher, gazed toward the horizon. "History was never our strong suit. We're spiritual people who rely on oral traditions. Did you know that Indians were one of the few cultures that never developed writing?"

Mira, intrigued, asked, "Why do you think that was?"

"It's likely because we didn't need it. Our lives were straightforward, uncluttered by large-scale trade or sprawling communities. But I'm digressing. I tend to wander sometimes."

Sofia refocused, her mind traveling back in time. "I think it's best to start with Alice," she began, settling into the flow of Hopi storytelling. "I was cleaning Chief Dan's house when someone came to tell him about a white woman sleeping in the park—the same place we met. It was 1957, the year I graduated from high school. I was a precocious sixteen-year-old, and Cheveyo was a couple of years younger.

"Chief Dan told me to bring her to his house. When I went to fetch her, she was barely conscious. She was likely a couple of years older than I was. Chief Dan, with his heart of gold, let her stay in his home. She was famished and didn't speak for a few days except to tell us her name was Alice, and she was heading to San Francisco.

"After a few weeks, Chief Dan asked my mom if Alice could stay with us until Cheveyo and his nephew could build her a small hut of her own. Mom agreed, but it wasn't easy. Alice would wake up screaming during the night. Something wasn't quite right with her. After it was built, she lived in her hut for the rest of her time with us."

"The same one you live in?" Alexi asked.

"No," Sofia smiled, "Cheveyo, I mean Lyam, built mine much later. Before Alice stumbled into our world, Lyam and I were living dream lives. Chief Dan had a great Tuuhikya medicine man teach us the ways of the Spirit. Cheveyo and I were fortunate because we were the children of Chief Dan's brother, so we were given all the perks of celebrity children. We learned about the healing powers of the native plants, fire ceremonies, tracking animals, and communicating with the spirit world. When Alice arrived, she absorbed the Hopi ways like a sponge, and the three of us spent lots of time together learning from each other. We often said we were learning the real 'facts of life' and then laughed.

"I still teach the old ways, but most Hopis aren't so interested. I try to blend the Hopi tradition with modern spirituality, but our tribe is very conservative—and I don't want to end up like Socrates," Sofia chuckled. "That's probably a lot for you to take in, right?"

"It is," Mira said quietly. "But how did Lyam end up here? And how did he and Alice get together?"

"Well, that's another story," Sofia stood. "Let's stretch a bit first."

As they did a version of 'rock' stretches, Sofia mused, "I love this place and wonder why I don't come here more often. Some find it dull, but when I look, as Chief Dan would say, 'with baby eyes,' I see its hidden beauty and forget about tomorrow or yesterday. It's a retreat from my doing-and-thinking world."

After a few more stretches, they returned to their sitting rock, and Sofia continued, "I don't know why it's so important to dig into the past, but I know it is in your culture."

"That's exactly what Alice says, '*Why dredge up the past?*'" Mira added.

Mira was eager to hear about Lyam. Yet, she felt this was

a rare opportunity to hear about Native American culture directly from a shaman. "Why do you think most Americans are obsessed with the past?"

"I'm always happy to share our culture," Sofia said with a smile. "European Americans look to the past for identity, analyzing mistakes and achievements, hoping to build a better future. Native Americans live in the present. It's all about harmony with nature and community, guided by spirit. Planning ahead? Not so much. Looking back? Hardly ever. Which is better? Neither. Each culture has its way."

Sofia paused, gauging Mira's reaction as she nodded slightly, then continued.

"Let's see… details about Cheveyo are like tracking a deer on rock." Sofia half-smiled. "He was born around 1943, back when skirmishes were still going on between the native people in northern Arizona and the immigrants."

"Excuse me for jumping in," Alexi interjected, "but I notice you use different names when referring to people like Mom and me—white people, Westerners, Europeans, immigrants… What does your culture prefer?"

"There's no one word fits all," Sofia replied thoughtfully. "It's the same with Native Americans, Indians, or Indigenous Americans. I don't lean one way or the other, so I use whatever comes to mind." Sofia looked at Alexi, then continued. "But around that time, many people—like you," Alexi grinned as Sofia gave her a playful wink, "were heading to California, chasing jobs. It was the tail-end of the Great Depression, and yeah, some came to Christianize the 'heathens.'"

"My uncle was Chief Dan, a beloved leader known for sharing traditional Hopi wisdom and prophecies," Sofia said, her tone shifting. "But every story has its shadow side. My father, Red Crow—Chief Dan's younger brother—was his opposite. Born shortly after the Civil War, he grew up on stories of conflicts with the white settlers. He held a deep-seated grudge, especially over the government's efforts to 're-educate' our children through missionaries—a dark chapter that lasted a century."

Mira's face fell, "I've heard about those horrible times. I can understand how Red Crow may have felt."

Sofia continued. "In 1895, Lomahongyoma, a Hopi chief, and eighteen others took a stand. They refused to send their kids to the government schools. Their defiance landed them in Alcatraz for nearly a year. My father admired him and would tell us stories about him."

"That's awful," Alexi said quietly. "I feel ashamed."

Sofia offered a consoling smile. "Don't be too hard on yourself. All cultures and organisms have their struggles. It's the nature of life. Either you resist and prevail or adapt and change. Some Native Americans wish we could go back to the days before Columbus. But really? I wouldn't. Life was relentlessly tough for most tribes, with constant battles for survival.

"From my studies in psychology, I've learned that dwelling on past abuses can ingrain these pains in the collective psyche of a culture. I teach that we should acknowledge the past but simultaneously understand it as another chapter in our cultural narrative."

Sofia's gaze softened, as if drawing from a quiet place within. "We can't let past atrocities define us. It's a difficult task, but I believe the healthiest approach is not to forget but to forgive and move on—not only for us but for our children."

Alexi hung on every word, "You sound so much like Lyam. Maybe you two *are* twins."

Sofia chuckled. "But let me continue. According to accounts from Chief Dan and my mother, a missionary family was driving west and stopped at our reservation to preach. My father, known for his temper, argued with them at their revival meeting. The next day, there was a terrible crash as they were leaving. People speculate there may have been a car chase. Maybe he tried to run them off the road. Whatever the case, both cars crashed and burned. My father escaped just before the cars went up in flames."

"I feel Lyam has something to do with this story," Alexi commented.

"Good guess." Sofia grinned. "Later that day, a passerby found Red Crow lying on the roadside and told my mother. When she got there, she found two charred cars. While helping my dad into the car, she heard a cry from a nearby bush."

Sofia glanced at Alexi. "Yes, it was one-year-old Lyam wrapped in blankets. He might have been thrown from the car during the crash, or, as my mother likes to tell the story, Red Crow pulled him out before it went up in smoke. My mother wanted a son, but not another child with my dad. My father died a week later, and she saw both events as a blessing from the Great Spirit. It was November 1944. I was almost three, and my sister was five years old. My mother got the son she'd always wanted, and I got a brother."

She paused before continuing. "The family's identification was lost in the crash, leaving the police with no clues. My mom never mentioned Lyam to the police. World War II and Christmas occupied everyone's attention, and the accident remains a mystery to this day. Lyam was left with no citizenship, no Social Security number, no identity."

"Or a citizen of nowhere," Alexi said, smiling at her mom before turning back to Sofia. "It's a joke from a book my mom read to me when I was a kid."

"I'm curious. How well do you know Lyam?" Sofia asked.

Alexi smiled, "He helped me grow up and sort out my confusion as a teen. I consider him my spiritual teacher and friend."

Sofia's face brightened, "Yes, I can imagine that."

"How did he get the name Lyam?" Alexi asked.

"Alice had something to do with that," Sofia replied. "Cheveyo was a couple of years younger than me, but had the wisdom of a shaman. Lyam and Alice were closely matched in that respect, but Lyam was in a league of his own. I felt he surpassed even the Hopi elders at the time. One day, we were tracking a rabbit. Lyam stopped and pointed to a track that neither of us could see. Alice laughed and asked him, 'Were you born on another planet? You're Light Years Ahead of everyone else.' That's how 'LYA' was born. His wisdom always amazed me. I suggested adding an m to his name when he left the rez to help him blend in."

"Lunch?" Sofia suggested.

Chapter 27

The Rest of the Story

After lunch, Sofia dove back into the story. The afternoon sun had invaded their space, so they found new rocks to sit on. "When Alice arrived, her reverence for our traditions was undeniable. It was as if she'd been searching for spiritual nourishment and was now being served the meal she'd been starving for. She dove into our way of life, soaking up new customs and ideas like a sponge, leaving her baggage untouched.

"Alice and I became friends, as much as she would permit. But it wasn't all smooth sailing. She seemed testy and closed. We never became as close as I'd hoped. I loved Cheveyo as a brother, but when Alice arrived, things got shaky. I could see Cheveyo falling in love with her."

Sofia paused, closed her eyes, and reflected on past feelings. "Was it jealousy? Confusion? I can't say. Alice never struck me as warm or compassionate, yet she became the golden girl for Chief Dan and Lyam. After the first year, I found myself stepping back, watching from the sidelines."

Sofia paused again, studying Mira as if trying to understand the relationship between Alice and her daughter. "But that's only half of it," she continued, her voice low and thoughtful. "After staying for two years, Alice suddenly announced that she was heading to San Francisco. I was secretly pleased, but Cheveyo was devastated. The next day, she got a ride as far as Las Vegas."

"Alice was born in 1940, so that would be 1959, when she was nineteen." Mira interrupted, thinking out loud.

"That sounds right," Sofia nodded. "Then, about three years later, Alice waltzes back into our lives and tells Chief Dan she wants to do a vision quest. I'm still in the dark about the whys and hows, but Chief Dan was happy to see her and had the shaman arrange one for her. We don't take those things lightly, so I was surprised about the whole thing. I never knew what was happening around Alice, but she was a charmer and knew how to get what she wanted. It took place sometime in the autumn of that year, and here comes the mysterious part," Sofia beamed as she looked at Mira. "Around nine months after that, you were born."

Mira chuckled, "Well, I *am* a doctor, so I believe we can rule out immaculate conception."

Sofia smiled, but her expression soon turned bleak. "There's a sad twist to this story. Two years after you were born, this guy, Ronald, shows up. He's a wiry, complaining fellow. After a few days, Kaiya announces she's heading back to San Francisco for a few weeks. It was the first time I overheard Cheveyo and Kaiya argue. She leaves you with Lyam and takes off with Ronald in his fancy green convertible.

"Alice doesn't return for another three-plus years. By then, you were almost six and the darling of the rez. I mean, with your blue eyes and blond hair! Some would call you 'white buffalo woman.' It was a contest to see who had the upper hand in spoiling you. And Lyam—he adored you. You two were inseparable. When Alice returned, she was wearing a hijab. Said she'd converted to Sufism, and she took you with her."

Mira was incredulous as the long-hidden details unraveled

before her.

"Just like that? Without a fight from Lyam?"

Sofia nodded dolefully. "I questioned him, and he showed me a letter from her lawyer, threatening arrest for kidnapping."

Alexi's voice cracked with shock. "Oh my god, she did that?"

"She held all the cards. Time changed her during those years away. She told Lyam that everything she did was in the name of love."

"Ouch. That hurts." After a heavy pause, Mira spoke softly. "I was only five, but I vaguely remember the lonely ride to San Francisco, not understanding what was happening. Alice told me to pack my stuff, but I had nothing to put them in except a few small boxes. Everything I knew, everyone I loved, was left at the rez."

"Was that the last time you saw Lyam?" asked Sofia.

Mira shook her head. "On my ninth birthday, I heard arguing in our living room. I peeked out my bedroom door just as a guy was rushing out of the house with a vitriolic Alice pointing the way. Later, Alice gave me a suitcase with a hidden compartment containing the poster I had stored in my trunk all these years."

"Interesting," Sofia commented, and looked at Mira. "Lyam left the reservation in 1972, a month after Chief Dan died. That would be a little before your ninth birthday."

Alexi wrinkled her nose and looked up as she crunched the numbers.

"I can see your disbelief, Alexi, but yes, Chief Dan did live to be one hundred and twelve. When Cheveyo left, it felt like a part of me went with him. I never thought I'd see him again."

The late afternoon sun nudged them again, this time to the shade of a lone piñon tree. Sofia continued, "In the meantime, I got my degree in American Indian Studies and delved deeper into our shamanic tradition. Then, out of the blue, Lyam reappeared."

"When was that?" Alexi asked.

"That I do remember. It was late August 1990, a week after my mother died. We timed his vision quest to end just before the full moon began to wane."

"We're talking early September, right?" Alexi clarified.

"That sounds right. When Lyam returned, he told me he had become a Buddhist monk but was called back to the rez to do a vision quest."

"Called? Lyam was called back?" Mira asked.

Sofia spoke slowly and deliberately. "There's a silent voice within, always speaking to us, but many are caught up in the endless buzz of our personal dialogues. I'm sure Lyam had plenty of time to listen at the monastery."

Alexi nodded, "Listening is his forte. Our times together are more silent than chatter. But one thing's bugging me. The dude who came to pick up Mom—Alice's boyfriend, I assume. Are we sure she and Lyam, you know… had a thing?"

"You'll have to ask one of them." Sofia chuckled." All I know is that after Alice's vision quest, she was beaming as if surrounded by invisible light. But after a few months, they became more distant. He became more introverted, and the most he said to me was, 'I made a big mistake.' Lyam always treated you as though he were your father," Sofia gazed at Mira. "Chief Dan told me that a vision quest is a powerful ceremony and that there are no mistakes when it's done in earnest, and he said Alice was very earnest. But back to Lyam. After his vision quest, he put on his backpack and walked into the mountains."

"I don't see any mountains around here," Alexi said as she scanned the horizon.

"To the west of here are the San Francisco Peaks. When we were teens, we would walk there, sometimes hitchhiking, and camp for several days. We loved that place. The Hopi have a legend that once, after a drought, they heard singing from the 'peaks.' Some Hopis went there to investigate and found Kachina spirits. The spirits returned with them and blessed their crops. That's the source of our yearly Kachina ceremonies."

They paused to watch a golden eagle circle above them—a rare occurrence for late afternoon.

"That reminds me to show you an eagle's nest nearby," Sofia said. "It's a good excuse to stretch our legs."

As they studied the nest, Alexi turned toward Sofia. "I'm trying to sort out Alice's comings and goings. You first saw her in 1957 when she was seventeen, right? Then she left the rez two or three years later and came back. When?"

"About three years later," Sofia replied. "She asked Chief Dan to guide her on a vision quest. Nine months later, your mom was born. Then, when Mira was two, Alice left her with Lyam and returned to San Francisco. She came back shortly before Mira's sixth birthday and took her from Lyam and the rez. Even now, that leaves a pain in my heart."

When they returned, they repositioned, like a game of musical rocks, dodging the sun's rays, and Sofia dove back into her story.

"When Lyam returned from San Francisco Peaks two weeks later, he was incredibly clear, as if he had shed his old larval self and emerged as a beautiful butterfly. I believe something amazing happened during his time in those Mountains, as if his personal identity had been deleted from his hard drive. He seemed to be carrying a secret he couldn't quite verbalize. We hung out together for a couple of weeks, one of the sweetest times of my life. Then one day, he told me that he was going to leave. Although our tribe doesn't get emotional or ask, 'Where are you going?' I did both. He said he'd gotten an assignment."

Alexi gulped as the realization snapped into place like a puzzle piece. "An assignment? And that was the same month I was born."

Sofia nodded as the meaning of 'assignment' finally sank in. "Lyam continues to mystify me."

After a pause, Sofia mused, "I love watching the sunset and clouds. When I look in a certain way, they always entertain me. It feels like a production put on only for my benefit."

Alexi grinned. "Lyam says the same thing—that the universe stages this grand spectacle for him alone."

"Let's watch it before we walk back," Sofia suggested, "If you're up for it, we can meet for a few hours tomorrow before you head back home."

"Yes, we'd like that," Alexi responded. "I have more questions, but they're all for Lyam."

Chapter 28

A Hopi Farewell

The morning was already warm by the time Alexi and Mira finished loading the car. They'd stayed up late, talking through the revelations of the past two days, which pushed their start later than planned. But before they left, a farewell meal awaited them with Sofia, their gracious host.

Stepping into Sofia's cozy home, they were greeted by the savory aroma that only a home-cooked meal can provide.

"Brunch, Hopi style," Sofia announced with a smile, gesturing toward the table—a vibrant spread of colorful dishes. Steam rose from the plates, promising a farewell feast to remember.

"Hopis are fond of squash and beans, but corn in all its glorious forms is our true Spirit," Sofia said, lifting a platter of piki bread, thin as secrets, made from blue corn and ash. "It's more than just food; it's a celebration."

Mira and Alexi settled into their seats, the mingling scents forming a kaleidoscope of warmth and comfort. Sofia bowed her head and spoke a few words in Hopi before looking up with a broad smile. "Please, eat!"

The meal unfolded like pages from a beloved book, filled with rich flavors and shared laughter. But as with all good things, there was a final chapter. After exchanging contact details, Sofia mentioned an almost forgotten custom. "Traditionally, guests bid farewell to the chief. I'll take you to Chairman Timothy's home for your goodbye."

They meandered along familiar paths, passing the grocery store and the small park where they first met.

"Last night, I had a vision," Sofia shared as they continued walking. "I was in a circle of twenty students, in the same place where we talked yesterday. A wise shaman draped in a white buffalo skin was teaching us. There was no doubt who that teacher was," she glanced at Alexi. "You were speaking in Hopi, and next to you was a scribe etching your words into rock tablets."

"That's interesting," Alexi said. "I've just started hosting meetings, but no one's chiseling what I say in stone."

Sofia laughed, "Interesting, to say the least. This world is a mystery, and my dreams are no less real than the three of us walking down this street."

"I remember reading about the Chinese philosopher Chuang Tzu," Mira interjected. "One night, he dreamt he was a butterfly. In the morning, he woke up wondering if he was a man dreaming of being a butterfly or a butterfly now dreaming he was a man."

"Exactly!" Sofia waved her arms animatedly. "'Is this a dream?' is the fundamental question that must be addressed before we can free ourselves from the grip of this world. And the only way to do that is to wake up as Lyam did."

Alexi nodded, excited that Sofia's understanding was similar to Lyam's. "Lyam talks to me about what you just said, and each time, I feel like I am getting it until I don't."

"I know what you mean," Sofia said warmly. "Talking about Lyam brings back memories I haven't touched in years. After his vision quest, he told me reality is not what we experience. A short time later, he said that reality is *only* what we experience. It took me years to untangle what he meant by that."

They walked in comfortable silence for a few blocks until Alexi asked, "Earlier, when we told you we enjoyed staying in our tent, you started to share your thoughts but left it hanging."

Sofia looked toward Alexi, squinting against the sunlight. "Let me ask you. Don't you find staying in a tent—liberating?"

Alexi's eyes lit up. "We so do. One night, we stayed in a hotel room because of a windstorm, and it was terrible. Besides the sheets smelling like a perfume factory, it was confining and suffocating."

Sofia nodded. "I like your choice of words, confining. That's how many Indian tribes felt when they moved from teepees to houses. For me, a teepee is not practical year-round. I admire my ancestors for being able to do that, but much of the joy fades when it's only for survival. When I camp in my little tent, it's a different story. I feel alive—energetically connected to the Spirit in a way that's hard to describe."

They arrived at Chairman Timothy's place, where Mira and Alexi said their goodbyes before heading back down the road. After a few steps, Sofia suddenly stopped and turned to Mira. "You came here to find where you were born, right? Let's go."

She led them along a dusty shortcut, and within minutes, Sofia stopped and extended her hand like a well-seasoned tour guide.

"A Gospel Church?" Mira's voice was a mix of confusion and humor.

"Mom, you were born in a church!" Alexi laughed.

Sofia joined the symphony of laughter. "Well, this is the ground you were born on. The church was built a few years ago. Things have changed since you were born. We have lots of steeples in this small town now."

As they headed back toward the car, Sofia turned to Mira. "I'm glad we took this walk—it got me thinking of something about Lyam. A while back, a guy came here asking for information. He said he worked for an elderly gentleman looking for your father. I told him about Lyam and how he'd returned to a Buddhist monastery near San Francisco."

"Interesting," Mira mused, more to herself than Sofia. "That's got to be Charlie's handiwork."

They arrived at their car in silence. "Well, Sofia, Mom and I are so very grateful. How do we say thank you in Hopi?"

"*Askwali*," Sofia responded in a soft, kind voice.

Alexi and Mira repeated, "*Askwali*," and bowed their heads in respect. They exchanged one last embrace. After a final smile, they slipped into their car, and Alexi set the GPS for the long drive home.

Chapter 29
Homeward Bound

It was quiet in the SUV, the radio long forgotten, as Alexi and Mira drifted in a sea of new revelations. Outside, heat waves distorted the Arizona desert. Alexi broke through the silence with a humdrum, dismissive tone, "Well, that was interesting."

Mira turned to her as laughter bubbled up between them, a release after the intensity of the last few days.

"Who would have thunk?" Alexi mused. "It's hard to believe Alice kept you in the dark all these years. I mean, what kind of person does that?"

"Your grandma," Mira replied.

Alexi laughed. "It all feels surreal. And this Lyam—"

"You mean grandpa," Mira cut in. The word sent a shiver down Alexi's spine.

"Light years ahead indeed," Alexi said wryly. "Our whole relationship has changed. I don't even know what to say to him now." She exhaled, trying to process her thoughts. "And you never heard Lyam or Lya at the reservation? Never saw him after he left the suitcase?"

Mira shook her head. "Remember what Sofia said. Lya was the name Alice gave Cheveyo soon after they met. When

Alice returned for her vision quest before I was born, Chief Dan told them the name Lya hurt his ears. After that, it was always Cheveyo. I believe I did see him on your seventh birthday, the first time I took you to the bike shop. He ducked into the back room as we walked through the door, and his helper waited on us."

"That I don't recall, but he was always there to help me. So, on two occasions, you only saw his back as he headed out a door?"

Mira nodded, "Alright, it's time for the rest of the suitcase story. Remember when Sofia mentioned I cried when I had to leave behind the poem Lyam and I wrote on birchbark with eagle feathers sewn in?"

Alexi's voice softened, "I do, which makes me sad."

"Losing that poem was the worst. But Sofia also reminded me of my leaf collection and the clothes she made for me. Alice was so hurried that she threw my stuff into three small boxes, saying we'd get whatever I needed in San Francisco. That must have been excruciating for Lyam to witness." Mira paused, placing her hand on her heart.

"It hurt when I couldn't see him again. But when Alice gave me the suitcase he'd left, I was too happy to ask any questions. I took it to my room and found a folded poster in a side pocket. At the bottom, it read, *To my lovely Mira*."

Alexi glanced at Mira. "Now I get it, the *Wherever You Go* poster. But I never noticed your name on it."

"That's because I erased it best I could. I didn't want Alice to see what he had written, but I would hang it on my wall..."

"Wherever you would go," Alexi interjected with a chuckle.

"Alice likely realized it was from him. The only concessions she made regarding Lyam were a suitcase and a poster. It reminded me of my wonderful times with Lyam and the tribe."

"But why was she keeping you from him? What's wrong with that woman? Why didn't Lyam contact you or tell me about all this? What is he doing in St. Cloud?"

"Hold on!" Mira lifted her hand. "I'm trying to sort it out too."

Alexi took a deep breath, letting the tension drain from her shoulders. "Sorry, Mom, but it's all so confusing." Alexi wished she could sometimes dial back her intensity and channel some of Mira's patience. She realized how overwhelming her barrage of questions might have felt.

Mira attempted to create a plausible plot. "Based on what Sofia told us, Lyam's hands were tied. Alice didn't want anything to do with him and, like Charlie, was tossed under the bus by an unstable woman. The full story? We'll only get that from Alice, which seems unlikely, or Lyam if he opens up. He may be in your life because he wants to connect with, perhaps, his only grandchild—if he is your grandfather."

"My grandfather," Alexi repeated. "That's not a word that flows off my lips. So, your only memory of him is his back?"

Mira's eyebrows furrowed. "Except maybe a few months before Alice came to get me when I was five. We were tracking a deer, possibly where we walked yesterday. A hawk swooped down, and as I backed up, I slid down a slope. Lyam knelt over me with tearful and compassionate eyes. I felt assured he would always watch out for me. Little did I know how true that would be."

"You remember all that?"

"I think so. But I know how the mind can fill in lost memories."

"What color were his eyes?" Alexi probed.

"Blue. But maybe that, too, might be my imagination, wishing to see a part of him in me."

"Yup, that's the color. They're hard to ignore."

"Other than that," Mira shrugged, "he's a mystery. Sofia told me I was born in the spring, which matches my birthday—April 5th."

"Well, damn, I don't know if I should hate him or… I mean, he's been such a lifeline for me."

"I suddenly find myself with a wee bit of time," Mira grinned as they crossed the boundary from the Hopi reservation into the Navajo Nation. "Give me some examples?"

"I'd love to," Alexi readjusted her seat, settling into her story. "Once, as we were floating in Lyam's balloon, he told me to see with different eyes. I said I could only see with the two eyes God gave me. Then, with a gentle tap between my eyebrows, he corrected me, 'God gave you another eye—see from there.' And just like that, the incessant chatter in my head fell silent. It was like stepping into a hollow and empty cave."

"And?"

"I get a bit emotional talking about this," Alexi admitted, pausing. "As I gazed at the landscape below—the colors, the cows, the kids waving at us—it felt stunning, like I was seeing the world anew. There were no thoughts or descriptions, just pure experience. Tears welled as I took in the barns and clouds against the most incredible blue sky I've ever seen. Lyam said I was now seeing things as they *were* instead of talking to myself about them."

Mira nodded, encouraging Alexi to continue.

"He also altered how I view situations as less solid and fixed. It's as though there's this usual me driving this car and talking to you, and then there's another version that's not physical or mental. It's this version of me that's unfrazzled and peaceful and makes what I do seem less important and inconsequential. I've changed over the years I have known him."

"Interesting. It sounds more mundane, less engaging with the world, a bit less interesting?" Mira challenged her.

"No, just the opposite," Alexi countered. "Now, whatever happens doesn't have the sting it did before. I still get upset at times, like after losing a bike race—after all, I've been practicing 'upset' since I was born. But I no longer indulge in it anymore.

I soon laugh at the absurdity and see it as another feature in my life, like my period. Constantly being upset was the boring part."

The dreary drive transformed as they swapped stories about Lyam, Alice, and Sofia. The sun dipped lower in the sky, signaling mid-afternoon, when Alexi spotted Gallup on the horizon. "Let's stop for gas. Anyway, rigor mortis is starting to settle into my legs."

With their food supplies reduced to crumbs, they found common ground at a *Subway*, agreeing on a foot-long to share at their next campsite. After a stroll past the glut of gas stations, they circled back to their car, and Mira took the wheel. The radio and her audiobook lost their charm as they agreed that car trips were ideal for in-depth discussions. With the recent revelations still fresh, Alexi couldn't seem to get enough. "You never knew Lyam was your father?"

Mira shook her head. "I still don't, and neither does Sofia. The day Alice whisked me to her place in San Francisco felt like stepping into a hurricane. Ronald, this tall, skinny guy, was jamming with his friends. He came over and scooped me into his arms. He reeked of booze and probably had no clue what 'bath' meant. He lived with us for a year, maybe two, and their fights were the soundtrack of my childhood. He introduced me to his friends as his daughter, so I honestly don't think Alice knew. Those years cost Charlie a fortune for my therapy bills." Mira chuckled.

Alexi pointed out a vibrant cluster of golden and orange cottonwoods as they continued westward, the leaves shimmering like tiny suns. Mira shared more stories about her time with Ronald and Alice—a series of anecdotes, none particularly rosy. She admitted, though, that Ronald's local fame had opened a few doors for Alice in the music scene.

Alexi's expression softened. "I can't imagine what that was like. How did you cope with it?

In these heart-to-heart moments with her mom, Alexi was in her element. Despite her lack of interest in psychology in college—perhaps because it was Mira's domain—she found herself drawn to it through her weekly meetings. Those gatherings weren't just philosophical roundtables but spaces for unguarded dialogue. Her knack for drawing out hidden emotions was a testament to her innate talent. Yet, her relationship with Alice remained a puzzle. She told her mom it was easier ironing out kinks in other people's lives, than her own.

Mira stared ahead at the endless horizon, then glanced at Alexi, "How did I cope? I've asked myself that many times. Being dropped into a new world was a culture shock. Indian children, including me, were schooled differently. My first year of school in San Francisco was a circus. I loved living on the reservation. It was like being cradled in a communal embrace. Everyone had a hand in raising me, and Lyam was my guiding light. He taught me so much."

"At five?" Alexi wondered.

Mira smiled as her thoughts drifted back to Lyam. "Not five. I started learning the Hopi way as soon as I opened my eyes. Lyam wasn't just teaching me traditions but connecting me to the Great Spirit. Sofia was like the mother I wished I had—and Lyam— he was the most doting and caring father anyone could ever imagine."

"So, those pictures of you as a kid in San Francisco dressed as an Indian—" Alexi looked at Mira with admiration.

"Yes, it wasn't for show. I *was* an Indian—a Hopi Indian. Our time in Hotevilla brought back feelings of how it felt to belong to the tribe. 'Hopi' means well-mannered and peaceful. I was lucky to be born on a Hopi reservation."

Alexi's expression shifted to concern. "Mom, have you noticed that noise in the engine? We're almost in Albuquerque. Should I book an appointment for tomorrow morning?"

Mira nodded. "Please do. It's getting late, so we should find a campsite anyway."

Chapter 30

Dodge City

The following day, Alexi and Mira found themselves in a dusty repair shop in Albuquerque. The air was a pungent blend of motor oil and rubber, contrasting with the homely scents of Sofia's kitchen the morning before.

Mira alternated between checking her watch and flipping through the *Albuquerque Journal* she found on a side table, wondering what the problem could be. Alexi scrolled through her phone, searching for campgrounds ahead. Mira's mood lifted as her car, now humming smoothly, rolled out of the shop—a simple fan belt issue, nothing more.

With the Sandia Mountains shrinking in their rearview mirror, they headed north on Interstate 25 toward the tail end of the Sangre de Cristo Mountains in Santa Fe. Alexi had already marked some campsites at the repair shop. "Mom, how about the Gunsmoke campground in Dodge City? It's seven hours from here, and it says they have clean restrooms and showers."

"Sounds good," Mira replied. "Maybe Marshall Matt Dillon will be our campground host."

She looked at Alexi, who was programming the GPS for their campsite. "Never mind," she chuckled, waving off Alexi's blank expression. "It's before your time."

Alexi slotted her phone and turned toward Mira. "I have a question."

"Only one?" Mira's smile lingered, a trace of relief after the mechanic's diagnosis: "Only a fan belt, ma'am."

"I keep wondering how you turned out so normal. Living with Alice must have been traumatic."

"You know," Mira began, "until we met Sofia, I never understood it myself. I feel fortunate. In my impressionable years, I was loved by so many—the tribe, Sofia, and especially Lyam. Alice, as you know, doesn't radiate warmth. Her style is more hands-off. But one thing I learned while living with her is that regret is the craziest of passions. Alice has been drowning in repressed anger and blame her entire life. Look what that's done for her."

Alexi reached over and touched Mira's leg. "If I haven't said it before, you're a wonderful mother."

A wistful smile crossed Mira's face. "Thanks, but it wasn't a cakewalk. I was tenacious and wanted to give you a normal childhood. 'Normal' still feels foreign to me. That's why I took so many psychology courses—to understand her and myself."

"Did it help?"

"I understood that Alice's self-worth wasn't tied to my happiness. It's easy to feel like a victim, but Sofia's stories about Native Americans changed my perspective. I sometimes worried I'd inherit her 'crazy' genes, but I learned those traits often skip a generation."

Alexi gulped as Mira raised a teasing eyebrow. "You're not like Alice, though in some ways you are—after all, you get your good looks from her. But from my own experiences—and a bit of psychology—I've come to see personalities in two ways: inspirational and nurturing. Inspirational types, like Alice, are energetic and driven, always working to shape the present to match their dreams. They have a charismatic charm and a knack for rallying others to their cause."

"Interesting," Alexi reflected. "What about the nurturing type?"

"Well, that's me," Mira said. "Nurturing personalities are more supportive and accepting. They are ready to listen and understand and are the epitome of patience and empathy. These traits have been my mantra as a mother."

After a pause, she looked at Alexi. "I'm curious, where do you see yourself on the scale?"

"Well, Duh!" Alexi smirked, resurrecting a word from her teen years. "You nailed me. I'm Alice déjà vu for you."

Mira smiled, "The same except for your formative years. You have an infectious energy that loves to initiate. Take your meetings, for example. You love your meetings, yet you're not interested in the day-to-day operations. Somehow, others do that for you. Your meetings and being single are a testament to your inspiration and determination to pursue your dreams. But you're balanced, unlike Alice, who's a goose egg on the nurturing scale. You're caring, and I believe you would be both grounding and inspirational as a mother."

"Whew," Alexi exhaled, taking it all in.

"But there was an upside to being with Alice. She would take me along on her adventures, so life was never boring. She was the ultimate flower child, a living embodiment of the counterculture. Think of the icons she crossed paths with: Timothy Leary, Ram Dass, Allen Ginsberg, and Abbie Hoffman. Ever read *The Electric Kool-Aid Acid Test*?"

"Ages ago. Was Alice on the bus or off the bus?"

Mira laughed, "She was so on the bus, she had a reserved seat. I tried writing about those wild times, but soon realized writing isn't my forte."

An hour north of Santa Fe, the landscape flattened out, dry and dusty like something from an old Western novel.

Pronghorn deer eyed them as they passed. Mira pointed towards the mountains on her left. "Somewhere in those mountains, I spent some fantastic years in my teens at the Lama Foundation. It was a crash course in Eastern spirituality mixed with a dose of teenage rebellion. That was the last time I was in New Mexico."

They exited Interstate 25 for Dodge City. It was a tad longer, but Mira's childhood crush on Matt Dilion, the TV Marshall who brought law and order to Dodge City, added spice to the long road ahead. After a quick grocery stop, Alexi took the wheel as their conversation ebbed and flowed with the landscape.

Every so often, Mira searched her phone for Hopi history, sharing what she found with Alexi. "Remember how Sofia told us how her father watched as their children were forced into those harsh boarding schools? This article talks about how men were forced to cut their hair, and were not allowed to wear traditional clothing. But the worst part is that they weren't permitted to practice their spiritual way of life. It was a seismic shift from how the Hopis had lived for centuries. I would've felt the same as Red Crow if I'd seen how the government treated his people."

"I do remember, and I was irate," Alexi responded. "But I noticed that Sofia didn't dramatize any of it. She talked about it without a hint of blame or accusation. I think she's an enlightened soul, and Lyam is lucky to have her for a *twin*."

"Absolutely," Mira agreed with a soft chuckle. "Quite a woman. I also found out that the U.S. government and some tribal members established the Hopi Reservation in 1882. But not everyone went along with it. A group called the 'hostiles' broke off and started their own village. Where do you think that was?"

"I have no idea,"

"Hotevilla. Hotevilla was a rebel community that didn't want to accept the settlers' cultural interference. They wanted to live as closely as possible to the traditional ways, which may be why Alice got expelled from the village."

Alexi turns to Mira, an unspoken invitation in the air.

"Once, at a peace rally, I heard Alice tell someone that when she returned to the rez, she started introducing hippie and Eastern spiritual ideas. That may have put her at odds with Chief Dan."

"Wow. Granny continues to surprise me." Alexi said with a chuckle.

"It's incredible, isn't it? Despite everything, the tribe accepted Alice, adopted Lyam, and treated me as one of their own. Imagine if Alice had taken me back to San Francisco right after I was born. I'd be a total mess!"

Mira and Alexi exchanged an easy laugh. "Okay," Alexi asked, "after all this, who do you think your father is?"

"Lyam," Mira answered without hesitation.

As the day wound down, the sky softened into shades of amber, casting a warm glow over the Kansas fields. It was the kind of evening that invited reflection. The shadows of cows stretching across the pastures sparked insight into Mira's darker parts. It was this balance of light and dark she was learning to navigate.

Her thoughts drifted to Lyam—her newly discovered father—and Sofia's stories of his wisdom. Gratitude welled up as she thought of how he'd shaped Alexi's, Sofia's, and her life. She reflected that every journey holds hidden depths if we're willing to investigate. Alexi's voice pulled her back to the moment.

"Are you as bummed as I am that tonight's our last night in our palatial digs?"

Mira smiled, grounding herself before she replied. "I'm glad we decided to visit the museum and Boot Hill tomorrow, even though we won't get home until well after midnight. Thanks for agreeing."

"You know how I'm looking forward to it," Mira said. "It'll be the perfect way to end the trip. But enough talk—I think I see Wyatt Earp up ahead, riding down Front Street."

Chapter 31

Ending a Promise

Alexi's trip to Hotevilla, then India, felt like a distant dream. The lush greenery of a rain-filled summer lay brown beneath a blanket of snow. Once pristine and white, it was now a dirty gray piled along the roadsides.

She pedaled past one of those piles on her way to the bike shop, locking her bike outside. Her cheeks, red from the cold as she stepped inside, welcomed by the familiar scent of chain lube. Lyam was standing behind the counter, talking with a customer. Alexi waved, and he smiled back. When the customer left, Lyam walked over to Alexi, idly flicking through a carousel of brightly colored bike bells.

"I have some news for you," Alexi hesitated, the words catching slightly. "Alice died yesterday."

The air became heavy for a moment as Lyam took in the news. His voice lowered, gentle and quiet. "I'm sorry. How are you and Mira coping?"

"Fine. As you know, we were never a close family. But it still stings. Death is a strange phenomenon."

Lyam nodded with an understanding smile. "It's a sunny day. How about a walk?"

They stepped outside, avoiding the slush. After a minute, Lyam began. "It's time to fill in some long-overdue gaps. Thanks for helping me honor Alice's wishes."

Alexi looked at him with understanding. "Can you start by telling me how you ended up in St. Cloud?"

"The short answer, Charlie," Lyam replied.

"Charlie!" Alexi repeated warmly. "Why am I not surprised? He's like some spirit that magically materializes in my family's life."

"I believe that could be the case," Lyam smiled. "All I knew about Alice was that she was from the Midwest. That was as much as she offered. After leaving the rez, I spent eighteen years as a Buddhist monk until I returned to do a vision quest."

"Sofia said it was September," Alexi said. "Like around September 5th, the day I was born?"

"I see you've already filled in some pieces." Lyam grinned. "After that, I returned to the monastery south of San Francisco, but nothing felt the same. A few months later, my Irish friend Conor and I left and wound up in Crestone, Colorado. In the spring of '95, this suit stopped by the site where we were remodeling a house. He said that Charlie had been tracking me down and wanted to come to Crestone to meet me."

Alexi and Lyam made their way to the banks of the Mississippi, now low and scattered with chunks of ice.

""Hmm," Alexi interjected. "Okay, we've got a good ferry named Charlie, a Buddhist Monk, and a mystery guy in a suit. Is this something from a novel, or the start of a bar joke?"

Lyam chuckled. "Well, you can add DNA to that list."

Alexi mimed jotting a note on a tablet. They laughed, and Lyam continued. "About five months later, in autumn—the most beautiful season in Crestone—Charlie flew out to meet me. On the first day, he asked if he could send my blood sample to New York for a paternity test. He'd gotten a blood sample from Mira the previous Christmas while they were in New York. I was fine letting science do its thing. I had zero doubts.

"While waiting for the test results, Charlie invited me to his favorite fishing spot in Montana. He hadn't been fishing in years, and tears streamed down his cheeks the moment he reeled in his first lake trout. What a wonderful week we spent together. Want to know how the test turned out?"

"No, not really," Alexi shrugged. "That's not important to me."

Lyam laughed, "Yes, I'm your grandfather."

Alexi breathed a sigh of relief, closed her eyes as tears welled up, and threw her arms around him for a long overdue familial hug.

Lyam waited until she'd regained her composure. "Charlie and I shared stories—mostly about your mom and Alice. He told me about meeting you in New York when you were a child. I talked about my years with Mira and how those years were the best of my life. Eventually, he discovered I didn't have a legal identity."

"I know, Sofia told Mom and me."

"I do now," I do now," Lyam said with a hint of pride. "I didn't need one at the monastery, and life with Conor was simple. He owned a truck and handled all the money for our carpenter gigs. Charlie said he would get me on the grid and help me get started financially if I ever wanted to come to St. Cloud to be with my family. I started to protest, but he cut me off, saying he figured that wasn't my style. 'Take it and make an old man happy,' he insisted, adding that he'd probably used up most of his time on this planet anyway."

"So that's how you were able to buy the bike shop?"

"He told me a bike shop in St. Cloud was the best investment he'd ever made." Lyam smiled at the memory. "We kept in touch until he died three years later."

Alexi kicked a chunk of ice off the sidewalk and watched it skid down the riverbank. "Oh, Charlie, Charlie! It's funny. I never knew much about him, but he was the glue that held our lives together." She paused. "So, when did you end up in St. Cloud?"

"About a year and a bit after I met Charlie. When I got here, I felt lost. I asked the universe for guidance, and one day, I saw you riding down the sidewalk on your little bike. A few days later, I noticed a *For Sale* sign in a bike shop window down the street from where you lived—if ever there was an omen. I sent pictures of you on your bike to Charlie. He thought you resembled him. Money and heart rarely go hand in hand, but Charlie had a gift for balancing both."

They wandered off the sidewalk and into the woods, leaving a trail of footprints in the soft snow. Their conversation flowed freely, pausing now and then to admire the ice sculptures drifting down the Mississippi.

"Will you be going to Alice's funeral? It's on March 6th," Alexi asked as they circled back to the bike shop.

"Yes, I will," Lyam assured her.

"Mom and I would like you to come to our house afterward for food and refreshments. Would you be okay with that?"

"More than just okay. I'm looking forward to it."

Chapter 32

Revealing Alice

It was one of those March days that tricks you into thinking it's spring. Alexi and Mira made their way to Alice's cabin, their boots sinking into the soft snow. Above them, icicles dripped from the porch roof, sparkling in the sun. As they opened the door, a rush of stale air greeted them, heavy with the sense of something that still lingered. Mira wrinkled her nose at the faint scent of death.

Alexi pulled Mira out of her thoughts. "Mom, I'm not sure how I feel about this. You?"

"It's strange," Mira's voice drifted through the cabin's stillness. "It feels like I'm standing at the crossroads, where the last traces of the woman who occupied so much space in my life are now gone."

Amidst the echo of their footsteps on the wooden floor, Alexi turned to her mom. "Remember, my book signing is the day before the funeral?"

"I do, but I probably won't be able to make it. This funeral is uncharted territory for me. There's so much to sort through."

"I understand. So do we have a game plan, or just wing it?"

"Hmm," Mira considered. "Let's divide and conquer—you

the kitchen and me the closet. Alice wasn't a pack rat, so it should all fit in the car."

As they placed Alice's life neatly into boxes, ready for the Goodwill Store, Alexi asked why Alice had opted for a Catholic burial instead of cremation.

"Alice's mother was a Catholic and was buried. But Alice wanting the same? That woman remains a mystery to me even in death."

As Alexi made several trips to the car, she reflected on the memories she had there as a child. After loading the last of Alice's kitchenware, she walked to the backyard, where the faint remnants of a fort she once built were barely visible. *When was that? Twenty years ago?* She smiled at the thought of Charlie's generosity as she moved a few rotting logs with her foot to where they should be. *Giving the cabin to Alice was just another thing Charlie did for her. Too bad Dad's Parkinson's is too advanced for him to enjoy it now.*

With the last of Alice's belongings loaded into Mira's SUV, Alexi commented, "It's surprising how simply Alice lived. Minimalism at its best. No frills, except for a little TV and those CDs of Minnesota bird calls."

"Alice would insist on calling them *birdsongs*," Mira corrected with a smile. "The last time I saw Alice alive, a loon started to wail. She looked at me and said, 'A spirit bird for me to follow! Oh, how loons thrill me.' It was as if she already had a foot in another world." Mira brushed her hands together. "Okay, I think it's a wrap. Let's lock up. I'll come back next week and do the cleaning."

"Mom, before we go, can you show me that secret drawer Charlie built into a wall?"

"Oh, I almost forgot," Mira thumbed her forehead. "It's a neat little nook where I used to stash buttons from the festivals Alice and I would attend. The lock is a knot in one of the pine boards near the right side of the fireplace."

Alexi felt around the wall. "Was Charlie into some serious espionage or something?"

"Here, push this knot," Mira said, taking Alexi's finger. "Then, tug the side like this."

With a satisfying click, the drawer sprang open.

"Whoa, cool. It's bigger than I imagined," Alexi marveled, peering inside. "What's this?"

She reached in and carefully pulled out a manuscript and a few worn notebooks, with a reverence usually reserved for an ancient text. "I'm blown away. Now I know what Alice was doing with her time."

"Not fishing," Mira quipped, her tone tinged with newfound respect.

Alexi flipped through the manuscript, settling on the first page. "All handwritten. *The Life and Secrets of an American Hippie* by Alice Armstrong. That's quite a title."

"Alice never did leave the sixties," Mira chuckled.

"Incredible," Alexi mused. "This must be about three hundred pages. Let me read the introduction."

The hippie generation wasn't just about drugs and free love. To be sure, there was plenty of both, but there's a side to it that has yet to be discussed. I was there from the beginning to the end. These are my personal experiences with many of the movers and shakers of that era, as well as high-profile individuals who shaped the lives of Americans—and the world.

Alexi paused, letting those improbable words from her grandmother sink in.

It was a wild mix of war, drugs, racial issues, and people in power who wanted more. It was a strange time, but isn't that what every generation says about their era? I have no wish to point fingers or settle scores. I only want to preserve the times I lived through with as much honesty and candor as possible. —Alice Armstrong.

Alexi stared at the manuscript, her mind whirling as she

reevaluated everything she thought she knew about Alice.

"This is surreal," she murmured. "It gives me goosebumps."

"I had no idea," Mira said slowly, mirroring Alexi's feelings. "All my visits… and always with her notepad. Maybe this was her way of showing who she truly was."

"Whew, I'm shaking inside." Alexi steadied herself, then noticed a bookmark tucked between the pages. "Look! I made this for her one Christmas. I traced Arlo and Zoe from the book and added your favorite quote: *Love and keep loving. Never accept no for an answer, and love will find a way through to the hardest of hearts.*"

"It's sad," Mira said softly. "I believe love didn't find a way with her because of her childhood wounds."

Alexi enveloped Mira in a hug.

As they left the cabin, manuscript in hand, Mira glanced at Alexi. "You have a gift for words. Maybe you can bring Alice's story to life."

Chapter 33

An Evening with Alexi

The room at St. Cloud State was buzzing with chatter fifteen minutes before the lecture was due to begin. Ellie, a 22-year-old sophomore, wished she had arrived earlier, but who would have thought this event would be such a hit? She was familiar with the lecture scene, where an empty seat was usually a given. When she spotted a couple of open seats in the aisle of the eighth row, it felt like striking gold.

Ellie had hoped to snag a front-row seat, eager to see Alexi up close and personal. When Alexi and her friend Suki were in high school, they created a class project that caught the community's attention—a twenty-minute video that blended biology with something more profound. It had lit up Ellie's classroom screen and sparked her imagination. Too bad that one parent's complaint on religious grounds led to it being removed from the curriculum.

Settling in her aisle seat now felt like a small victory. Besides, sitting between fragranced people tested her patience. A voice broke through her thoughts. "Is this seat taken?"

"No, it's all yours," she replied, glancing up to see a guy sliding into the seat. "I'm Michael," he introduced himself.

"I'm Ellie." She discovered she was no longer interested in

the magazine on her lap and surreptitiously glanced at his profile. *Well, this is good luck—no smells, and he's pretty good-looking to boot. I like the cool cap, but that sweater has got to go. I wonder if he's the one. Damn, did I just think that? I mean, come on, Ellie.*

She'd been practicing mindfulness meditation for over a year and had gotten good at observing her thoughts and emotions beyond her meditation cushion. *Maybe Mr. Pike was onto something with his theory about primitive survival instincts shaping interactions between men and women.* She recalled how he explained it in anthropology class—how, in the first moments of contact, the brain makes swift, unconscious calculations. Every word and thought that follows is merely a disguise for one fundamental question: Would this person be a desirable mate?

Okay, maybe I was a little high at the time. Ellie's thoughts cascaded. *But I got it on a deep level. Should I say something to him? Once the lecture starts, it'll be too late. No, I'll see if he says something first. Oh, but he introduced himself. And like my mom says, if you don't put yourself out there. Okay, here goes.*

"So do you..." Ellie and Michael's words did a tango mid-air, and they shared a nervous laugh. With a casual wave, Michael gestured for her to go first.

"Thanks, Mike. I was going to ask if you go to school here because I've never seen you before."

"I do. But I prefer Michael. I'm not a fan of Mike," he corrected politely. "I'm working on my coaching degree in wrestling, so it's not likely we share the same classes. I was going to ask if you knew what this lecture was about."

Ellie's voice spiked with disbelief. "You don't know, Michael-not-Mike?" she teased. "So why are you here?"

"I planned on attending a karate meet-up next door, but it got axed. Thought I'd check this out for a few minutes," he shrugged.

"You don't know anything about Alexi?" Ellie asked. She held up her copy of *Who Am I?*, hoping to get it signed, and pointed to the images of Arlo and Zoe on the cover.

"Afraid not," Michael admitted, looking at the whimsical drawings of Arlo and Zoe. "This a comic book or something?"

Ellie smiled, "As they say, you can't judge a book by its cover. It's a fun book, but more than you'd suspect. But I'm sure Alexi will describe it better than I could."

"I'm guessing you're really into this guy."

Ellie grinned, happy to discuss the book and its author. It was what got her interested in meditation. "Totally. But Alexi is a woman, and something of a saint to me. There are rumors that she hosts weekly meetings."

"Meetings about what?" Michael leaned in, possibly more intrigued with Ellie than the book.

"I heard her say in an interview that her meetings are about the 'facts of life.'" Ellie noticed his grin and thumped the book on his leg. "Not *those* facts of life, but the real stuff, like why we're here and what really matters in life. I hear she's a pretty powerful lady."

As Alexi entered, Ellie wrote her name and phone number on the inside cover and handed the book to Michael. "Here, read it, and then let's meet for lunch. I would love to hear what you think."

Alexi stepped onto the stage in a stylish pantsuit that blended shades of earth tones and Native American jewelry. She surveyed the room, then smiled as the audience settled into their seats. "Hello, I'm happy to welcome you all. Can everyone hear me, or do I need a mic?"

Ellie leaned over with a mischievous smile and whispered, "She means she might need to use a Michael."

Michael choked back a laugh. "Okay, I owe you for that." Still chuckling, he delivered a slow karate chop into her ribs. With that, she knew they were going to be a couple—unless one of them blew it.

Chapter 34

No Mistake

Dark clouds hung low as Alexi picked up Mira for the drive to the cemetery. A comfortable silence settled between them, shaped by years of shared history and unspoken understanding. After a while, Mira broke the silence, asking about Alexi's event from the night before, a hint of regret in her voice for having missed it.

"The talk went well," Alexi nodded. "It was interesting, though. After the book signing, a small group kept hanging out and asking questions. I felt like the character in the movie *Being There*—about the gardener everyone thinks is a wise sage."

"Ha," Mira chuckled.

"All were sweet and sincere—especially a girl called Ellie and her boyfriend. Everyone appeared to be committed to self-discovery and willing to do what it takes to gain a deeper understanding of themselves. At eleven, the janitor put an end to it."

Mira smiled, "Did you tell them about your Friday meetings?"

Alexi shook her head. "Steve's living room is already overflowing, but I suspect Ellie will find her way there. She seems very determined."

"Thinking of a bigger space?" A suggestion Mira had made before.

"I hope it doesn't come to that," Alexi responded, unsure if she meant it. "Oh, Suki was there and sent a hi to you. It was sweet to see her again."

The cemetery gates came into view, and their conversation faded into a shared, quiet reflection on Alice's life. The cold air underscored the finality of the day, yet carried a quiet, unspoken hope. Alice's legacy was still unfolding, and the manuscript she left behind held the potential to change lives.

"Ah, Lyam." Alexi nodded at the familiar figure standing next to his pickup truck.

Mira smiled when she saw him. "I'm glad we stopped by his shop so I could personally invite him for brunch. I admit, I was shaking when we met."

"Don't forget the tears," Alexi added.

"Long overdue," Mira admitted. "Not many people would keep a promise like that."

Stepping out of the car, Lyam immediately wrapped them in a warm embrace, his down coat the only barrier between them. After the funeral and laying Alice to rest in the frozen Earth, they gathered at Mira's house. What began as a quiet brunch gradually turned into a lively exchange of stories and memories. The shift to Mira's living room was seamless, the steaming teapot of ginger tea felt part of the shared experience.

"Who would've thought?" Alexi smiled and lifted her cup in a playful toast. A warm sense of contentment washed over her.

Mira's months of mulling over the mysteries surrounding Lyam were finally unraveling. "Sofia told Alexi and me how your vision quest changed everything for you. Can you tell us about that?"

"I'd be happy to." Lyam's voice carried warm memories. "While at the monastery, I felt this urge—perhaps like birds have when they know it is time to fly south—to do a vision quest. I believed I would wear a monk's robe for life, but my life started to feel lopsided—too much heaven, not enough earth. I was trading one kind of attachment for another—exactly what Buddha warned us about."

One night, I had a vivid dream and sensed Alexi." Lyam looked at Alexi with warmth that brightened the room. "I didn't understand it, but knew I had to return to the rez.

"During the vision quest Sofia guided me through, the fog lifted. I reexamined my life and realized it didn't matter what path I chose—life is life. It became clear that my mission wasn't to sit on my bum all day pretending to like every monk at the monastery." Lyam chuckled.

"That vision quest and two weeks on the San Francisco Peaks became my wake-up call. I knew what I had to do. And I was lucky because what I had to do is what I *wanted* to do."

"So, in a way, you helped birth me," Alexi said with a thoughtful smile.

"I believe that is the case—energetically speaking. But you also birthed me because I was a new man after that."

Their conversation wasn't the usual parlor room banter. The air felt charged, as if it could realign the Earth's magnetic poles. A brief silence settled before Mira turned to Lyam.

"I wonder how you managed to keep your promise to Alice. Did you resent her for it?"

Lyam's gaze drifted to distant memories. "I did, for years. Every time I thought about what she did to me—what she did to you—I was filled with bitterness and blame.

"During my vision quest, everything shifted. I could no longer resent others because there were no others. I saw everyone as myself. That insight transformed my resentment into a deep peace that couldn't be disturbed, no matter what the world threw at me."

As the sky glowed with reds and warm oranges, Mira and Alexi walked Lyam to his pickup.

"I always hoped," Mira said quietly, the sunset reflecting in her eyes, "that Alice would wake up one day and talk to me like a real mother."

"But she *was* the perfect mother." Lyam's voice was infused with years of wisdom. "Look at you. Look at Alexi. Do you think this happened by accident? Still, she remains a mystery to me. My mind wants to believe that reconciliation or redemption should mark the culmination of a life. Then again, there is no end to life. Beneath her brokenness, Alice's essence is still as pure as this fresh snow. Who's to judge?"

He paused, then pulled Mira and Alexi into a warm embrace. As they stepped back, he looked at each in turn. "One thing's for sure—this was no mistake."

Part III:
Within and Beyond

Chapter 35

On the Air

"Alexi, good to go?" Lenny fired off the question with a smile as his fingers darted over the maze of buttons and dials at his radio station.

Sitting comfortably on a stool in WTMF's soundproof booth, Alexi surveyed the room—foam walls soaking up the sounds and screens quietly blinking. "I'm so ready."

"Welcome to our show, everyone!" Lenny began. "We've got something special for your ears on this rainy summer day. Joining us is Alexi Aguero, whose book, *Who Am I?*, is causing quite a stir among parents and teachers in our area. Alexi, what's up with that? What's your secret sauce?"

Alexi leaned into the mic, "Honestly, Lenny, it's somewhat of a fluke. I was a middle school teacher here in St. Cloud, and during that time, I was pedal-deep into bike racing. I spent a lot of time at Lyam's bike shop, just down the street from my mom's house." As Lenny listened, Alexi recounted the pivotal moments that led up to the present: the book's mysterious arrival in the mail when she was a teen, the balloon that almost flew away, and her transformative visit to Hotevilla.

"That's an incredible story," he remarked as he set his coffee cup on the table and readjusted his headphones. "So, you only made some edits and additions to the book? Lyam wrote the original?"

"That's right. Lyam's a private, down-to-earth guy who prefers avoiding the spotlight. He didn't want his name listed as the author, and as you're aware, Lenny, he declined your invite to be on your show. He's more of a one-on-one guy."

"It's truly amazing that he's your bike mechanic *and* your grandfather."

"Oh, Lyam's more than that. He's also my cycling coach and spiritual mentor—kind of a dream grandfather," Alexi answered, her smile and warmth likely felt by the radio audience.

"Sounds like a Swiss Army knife of a granddad," Lenny chuckled. "Did you ever think your book would be such a hit?"

"In one word—no," Alexi shook her head. "But I think the book and video work well together."

"A video? Can you tell us more about that?" Lenny prompted.

"I teamed up with Suki, my best friend from school, for a class project at Apollo High. We put together a 20-minute video based on Lyam's book to make it both engaging and educational for students. Somehow, it aired on Saint Cloud University TV, and before we knew it, biology teachers started using it in their classrooms."

"Interesting! After my twins read your book, I picked it up and was surprised by how much I enjoyed it—I didn't want it to end!"

Alexi smiled. "Thanks! Yeah, it's a quick read but a good way to introduce a fresh perspective on life without being preachy. My mom read Lyam's book to me during my angsty teens. It had a transformative impact on my life."

Lenny flipped through his notes and picked a quote from the book. "I was particularly struck when Kay tells Arlo that when he finds the love inside, the outside will love him back.

Mind unpacking that for us?"

"Absolutely. That's the heart of the book. It's not about searching for love in an activity or a relationship—that's a Band-Aid, right? The love we're looking for is built into our DNA. Once we discover peace and love within ourselves, relationships improve, and the world is all too eager to love us back."

Lenny shook his head. "That stopped me when I read it. I realized it's not just a kid's book. On a different note, what is the most important lesson Lyam taught you?"

Alexi's expression softened. "He used to tell me, 'Silence speaks for words unsaid.' He'd take me on balloon rides and we'd spend hours floating above the fields, watching the clouds—never saying a word."

"Huh. In radio, we call that dead air," Lenny chuckled. "Speaking of filling the air, we have several questions from the audience. Feel like tackling some?"

Alexi smiled, "Sure, bring 'em on."

Lenny scrolled his screen, "We have a couple of questions asking if you're a 'guru.'"

"I've been called worse," Alexi laughed. "The word 'guru' has evolved here in the West. There's a tech guru, a tool guru, even a food guru. I call Lyam my bike guru. In India, a guru helps you see your true nature, like how Kay guides Arlo in the book. Kay and I say no one can teach who you are inside—it can only be pointed to. So, I'm not a guru—more a 'pointy' person."

Lenny chuckled. "On that note, Andrew asks, 'Was there a moment when you knew you were meant to be a spiritual teacher?'"

Alexi paused, caught off guard. "Hmm. I've never considered myself a spiritual teacher. But I believe Andrew means having weekly discussions about life's most fundamental questions. From that perspective, I don't think there was a single event—more like a series of moments that only connect when I look back. Like painting a picture of myself, bit by bit."

"Nicely put," Lenny said as he scanned his screen. "Winona, one of your former students, wants you to know how much she loved having you as a teacher."

"Sweet! Thanks, Winona. I loved having you as a student."

Lenny scrolled through more questions, many circling the topic of religion. He picked one marked anonymous. "Someone asks if this is a religion. They mention that you lead meditations at your meetings."

Alexi shook her head. "No, not a religion. We usually start with a mindfulness meditation to help everyone unwind after a busy week. It's the same kind of meditation thousands of doctors recommend for reducing stress and anxiety."

"As a fan, it's hard for me to be objective," Lenny admitted. "But after my kids read your book this winter, we noticed a positive shift in both of them. And Timmy's grades even improved."

"That's great to hear, Lenny! Tell them I say hi and to keep up the good work."

"I will!" Lenny chuckled. "Well, Alexi, I wish we had more time, but before we wrap up, do you have any final thoughts to share with our audience?"

"Yes, I do." Alexi paused thoughtfully. "Our gatherings in St. Cloud may not be for everyone. In every society, there are those who feel something's missing and set off on a personal quest, like Arlo in the *Who Am I?* book. He felt an urge to seek something beyond the usual path of family and job. Then, a chance encounter with Kay sets him on an inward journey, more daunting and rewarding than the adventure he began with Zoe. During their adventure, Arlo discovers that what he was looking for wasn't 'out there,' but within, quietly waiting to be seen.

"Our weekly meetings build on this idea: it's not about having more to make us happy—it's about uncovering parts of ourselves that don't need more. Before Arlo or anyone else can fully enjoy life, they first need to make friends with who they are inside—the place where love, joy, and peace already reside."

"Thank you, Alexi, for that insightful interview. And to all of our listeners, tell your friends that you heard it on *Lenny's Listen and Learn* WTMF, St. Cloud."

Chapter 36

Problems

The last rays of sunlight streamed into the room through the large west window, casting warm golden patterns over the faces gathered for Friday's meeting.

"Welcome, everyone," Alexi's voice broke the quiet after the usual 15-minute meditation. Thirty or so attendees shifted positions, slowly opening their eyes.

Carol was the first to speak, "This is our fifth meeting with you, and every time, on our drive home, Henry vents his frustration with a litany of reasons why you just don't get it. He keeps saying you're..."

"It's all right, you can say it," Alexi reassured her.

Carol drew a breath, "Okay. Henry says you're a Pollyanna, and he doesn't want to come back—yet here we are. I like your meetings but agree with him on many of his points."

Alexi directed her attention to Henry. "Henry, would you feel comfortable sharing your concerns?"

Henry, never shy in a conversation, quickly agreed. "Certainly. I'm a counselor at the University of Mankato, and every day, I encounter a wide range of problems. Students are distressed by social and racial injustice, climate change, and world hunger, the same issues I worry about. What bothers me is that you don't discuss, but rather dismiss, these issues. You bag them up and say they're merely illusions."

"I see," Alexi calmly responded. It was not the first time she heard similar concerns. "It's not my intention to minimize the gravity and distress of these challenges. During our teatime, following meetings, we sometimes discuss problems the world abounds in. But let's make it personal and talk about your situation. Would that be okay?"

"Sure," Henry agreed, relieved to address his frustration with Alexi instead of complaining to Carol.

Alexi met Henry's eyes. "From our previous exchanges, it seems you see the world as flawed and believe these problems must be solved to create a better world. But as long as you see them as negative or the world as broken, problems will continue to plague you. I suggest you reshape your statement and use the word 'challenges' instead of 'problems.'"

Henry's brow furrowed. "I don't get it. Just changing the word won't change the situation."

"Oh, but it does," Alexi said. "It might sound trivial, but words shape how we see the world. They have the power to move mountains. Often, life's challenges instill in us a desire to awaken from our dreams, instead of believing that the world is the cause of our well-being.

"But they're still here no matter how I reshape the word," Henry persisted.

"Okay, look. I agree that climate change and social inequality are integral to the fabric of life. If this meeting occurred at the United Nations, we'd discuss problems and how to solve them. But in this setting, rather than focusing on problems and solutions, your attention is directed to the source of everything that happens in your life. Did you read Lyam's and my book, *Who Am I?*"

Henry shook his head.

"It's okay. In the book, Arlo is asked to look within, beyond his problems and complaints, to the source of intelligence and creativity—it's a good read, by the way," Alexi added with a smile. "As you tap into this inner reservoir, your life naturally aligns with nature. Let this be your challenge: build your house on the foundation of love and joy. Only then will you be ready to meet life's problems."

"You mean that we'll all live happily ever after." Henry's words dripped with sarcasm.

"I do mean that," Alexi replied, "but I can tell by your tone that you might not understand what I mean by 'joy.' Joy doesn't mean never having a car accident, never arguing with Carol, or ignoring concerns about climate change. This is not that kind of world. We live in a world of differences, good and bad, blended in a sea of gray.

"Joy isn't about avoiding difficulties or sidestepping obstacles. It's about facing them without letting them take the wheel. It means staying anchored in inner peace, no matter what the world tosses our way—recognizing that the highs and lows are just surface-level minutiae. A guru once told me that once we understand this, we can begin living 200% of life."

Henry's job revolved around helping his students deal with or eliminate problems. He shifted in his seat, frustration creeping into his voice. "I understand that inner peace is part of the equation, but problems don't just vanish."

"In a way, they do," Alexi replied, recalling how difficult it was when Lyam first explained this to her. "These meetings aren't about fixing problems—they're about waking up to a higher reality, seeing life from the mountaintop instead of being stuck in the valley."

"So, we ignore problems and live like monks?" Henry persisted.

"Not at all. I mean, monks have such boring wardrobes," Alexi quipped and heard some giggles, but Henry's expression remained unchanged. "Ignoring issues still isn't looking in the right direction," she continued. "I'm suggesting you look to that silent area within. That's where your treasure lies, untouched by worldly problems. Obstacles and challenges still exist, but they won't overwhelm you. Beneath it all is a substratum of peace and joy, a presence you can almost sense. When this becomes your reality, it's a true two-for-one. A joyful counselor makes for a wiser guide."

"But when I go home, problems are still there, waiting," Henry insisted.

Alexi paused. "When I was a kid, we had an attic full of Mom's old hippie stuff. One of my favorites was a poster from the '80s—a guru wearing a dhoti, Rudraksha beads around his neck, and standing on a surfboard riding a giant wave. It was an ad for a meditation lecture in Santa Cruz. The caption read: *You can't stop the waves, but you can learn to surf.*"

She smiled at the memory. "There will always be waves testing our balance, and we can't avoid getting wet. Every organism has two tendencies: one that lands us in trouble and one that gets us out. It's like music: dissonance makes harmony more interesting. A life without challenges would be dull. If we solved all our problems, we'd face an existential crisis—what would be left to do? Problems can frustrate us or point toward our true nature."

Henry nodded slowly, his voice becoming more conciliatory. "It sounds like the razor's edge."

"I'm not a fan of the phrase," Alexi said with a smile. "That sounds so sharp and treacherous. Sure, it's challenging, but not in the way 'the razor's edge' implies. It's not about renouncing the world, living like a monk, or shunning social activity. Lyam often talks about this. He says that getting attached to renunciation and spiritual practices is as entangling as being attached to the material world."

"Like desiring in reverse?"

"Exactly! If your passion lies in social work or teaching, go for it. We all have our roles in this worldly drama. Take me, I'm a middle school teacher, and trust me, there's a lot of social work needed in that field. What we talk about in these meetings isn't about what you do or the sacrifices you make. It's about seeing beyond or through surface-level issues to the reality that lies within while fully engaging in life. The way to change the world is to change yourself."

Alexi paused, then playfully asked, "How ya doing, Henry?"

He gave a faint smile. "Your message isn't exactly what most people are used to hearing."

Alexi's voice softened. "This is the root of so much madness in the world. It's like battling a many-headed hydra—solve one problem, and two more appear. But once you truly grasp this, your perspective shifts. Problems start feeling less like obstacles and more like challenges. Life shifts from a burden to an adventure. With this shift, a newfound joy arises that enriches your experiences and relationships and elevates everyone around you."

"Thank you," Henry responded slowly. "I kind of get it."

"Well said," Alexi nodded in agreement. "I'm in the same boat. Conversations like ours seem graspable, but they're only 'understood' beyond the limits of the mind."

Alexi looked out the dark window at the glow of the crescent moon, smiling in on the group. "I think this is enough for tonight—perhaps too much. Ellie, any announcements—or problems?"

Chapter 37

Move the Gloves

"Welcome, everyone," Alexi began the meeting with a relaxed smile. "Last week, we discussed approaching problems from a different perspective. Our site got half a dozen questions and comments on this topic. Let's see if we can clear the fog a bit."

With a half-serious tone, Andy, the drama coach at St. Cloud State, chimed in. "I was here last week and left with a new set of problems."

Alexi smiled, "This is the *problem* with our discussions; you must check your logical mind at the door. Socrates would be at home here. But logical Aristotle? He'd be scratching his head. We're here to touch the intangible, to understand that which defies the straight lines of logic. The thinking mind gets lost here."

"Sounds like a maze with no clear exit. So why come here?" Andy continued, playfully scratching his head.

Alexi chuckled, aware of Andy's flair for the dramatic. "There are levels of the human body that are intelligent in ways your rational mind can't begin to comprehend. It's these aspects that 'get' what happens here."

"So, we can absorb this through osmosis?" Andy's tone was humorous, hardly expecting confirmation.

"Osmosis," Alexi repeated with a thoughtful smile. "Interesting choice of words. It's like that, but more of a nonverbal vibration that stirs subtle aspects within us, particularly finer levels of the nervous system."

Andy's usual glibness gave way to seriousness. "My therapist says emotional traumas are stored in my body. Do conversations like this help?"

"I believe they do," Alexi responded, happy this question arose. "Emotional traumas can control our lives. The body can 'hear' this message energetically."

"So, do you recommend therapy?"

"I do," she replied without hesitation. "My grandmother was a trauma queen and carried her pain to the grave. Over the years, I've found that realizing Being, who you truly are, needs an unencumbered place to land."

"I get it," Andy added. "My wife's friend prides herself on her spiritual insights, yet her life is a constant dumpster fire."

Alexi chuckled, "Ha, that's good. Our gatherings are about awakening to your true nature. For many, being in a group enhances this understanding. Our energy reaches beyond the physical body, shaping and influencing the world around us. Without a deep understanding of who you are, there's always that sense of something being off, like a car engine that's out of sync."

"Hmm, thank you," Andy mused.

The conversation lulled until Donna picked up the thread. "My friends sometimes call me a space head, but I kinda get what you're getting at," Donna smiled at her clumsy choice of words. "I've been coming to your meetings for a couple of months, and I'm still baffled when you say things like 'know your essential self' or 'realize your true nature.' Before coming here, I'd never heard those phrases."

Alexi nodded. "I was fourteen when my mom read me, *Who Am I?* Before that, I never questioned who I was, because

I thought I knew—but not. Who I thought I was was a far cry from what that book hinted at."

After hearing Alexi's recent radio interview, Donna felt a surge of hope. A renewed sense of purpose stirred within her for the first time since her accident. Inspired, she realized her life wasn't defined by her wheelchair but filled with untapped potential.

Donna raised an eyebrow. "It was that book? I read it, and I'm not close to knowing this."

"Know this?" Alexi leaned forward. "No one can—not really. Even the Buddha said as much. That's why there are mountains of Buddhist texts, all skirting around the truth. What we're talking about here isn't something you grasp with your mind or put into words—it can only be realized or 'known' outside time, space, thoughts, and a personal me. The book *Who Am I?* sparked my search, but it was Lyam who became my guiding light."

"So, it was the book—and Lyam?"

"Indeed, I owe my transformation from a rebellious teen to who I am now entirely to Lyam." Alexi smiled, reflecting on her journey over the past fifteen years. "On our many bike and balloon rides together, he opened my mind to possibilities beyond the familiar—and I was hooked. Lyam nudged me toward a Buddhist retreat, eventually leading to a year in India. There, I sought out every spiritual teacher I could find."

She took a deep breath. "Yet, true awakening—the moment of seeing who I truly am—came much later, during a silent retreat in Massachusetts. In that stillness, the ground beneath me vanished, and I fell into a void—a space of pure Being, where the illusion of separation dissolved into oneness."

Whew!" Donna shook her head slowly. "Seeing from being? I can't even begin to imagine that."

Alexi's voice remained steady, "But you already do, Donna. Being is all there is. However, our minds often obscure that truth. It's like a prism scattering pure white light into different colors. We get caught up in the colors—the shifting forms and experiences—and mistake them for reality. In the end, it's all the formless light of Being. Did that help?"

"Hmm," Donna murmured, "I'm not sure because it seems there's a difference between how we perceive things."

Alexi nodded thoughtfully. "We see the same world," she clarified. "The difference is in what is 'seen' beyond the surface level. Imagine walking into a room and seeing a man bound in chains, submerged in a glass tank. Your reaction might be horror, believing it's real. But to the audience, it's just a performance—an illusion. Our 'understanding' shapes our perception of the world."

"How can I eliminate my mistaken beliefs and realize what you are saying?" Donna probed.

Alexi shrugged, yet there was wisdom in her casual gesture. "I can't tell you how, but I can tell you it doesn't start with giving up beliefs—that's a by-product. Different teachers say different things. Some advocate working hard and persisting; others claim nothing can be done, and even giving up is futile."

"What do you say?" Donna asked bluntly.

"I say it's not about changing your beliefs but noticing without attachment. When you observe without judgment or the need to change what is, beliefs begin to lose their grip. In that open space—free of beliefs and mental investment—truth reveals itself."

Alexi paused, searching her mental archive, "But above all, I say 'intend.' It's the intention to know the truth. Intention itself becomes your guiding beacon."

"And you say that realization happens if one intends?" Donna persisted.

"I don't know. It's a mystery that somehow, sometimes, happens. But after being around Lyam for years, I knew I wanted what he had. For me, it was intent, but this shift of perception also happens to those who don't intend. It's all pretty crazy."

Donna raised an eyebrow. "Intend? That's it?"

"Intend first, then investigate." Alexi hesitated, wondering if she should say more, but merely added, "Question the life you are now living."

"You mentioned you spent a lot of time meditating." Donna's inflection implied a question.

"Yes. Meditation helped me quiet my busy mind and appreciate the finer levels of Being. But for some, their proclivity is selfless service or love of the divine. There's no 'one-size-fits-all' formula. To say more would only expand your conceptual world and give you more beliefs to cling to. Grace, your essence, will provide the way."

Sensing the conversation was coming to a close, Donna offered a simple, sincere "Thanks."

After a pause, Alexi shared a personal anecdote, "My dad enjoyed watching boxing matches on TV. One evening, as I walked through the living room, the commentator pointed out that the fighter favored to win was losing because he was waiting for the perfect punch. He suggested that if the fighter simply started moving his gloves, the perfect punch would eventually come."

Donna's eyes lit up, "I like that. My husband loves boxing but is terrible at making decisions. So, start moving the gloves; there's no secret?"

"In a way, there is a secret. The secret is so simple and obvious that it's overlooked." Alexi paused for a second before continuing, "A border guard noticed a man crossing from Mexico to California daily with a wheelbarrow full of sand. Despite checking every day, the guard could only find useless sand. On the guard's last day of work, he asked the man, 'I know you're smuggling something, and because I am retiring today, could you please tell me what it is?' The man replied, 'Wheelbarrows.'"

Chapter 38

A Gathering of Minds and Hearts

Alexi's living room was buzzing with energy as the six core members of *The Meetings* settled in, filling the space with conversation and laughter. Julie's lighthearted voice cut through the chatter. "Okay, let's hit the pause button."

Heads turned her way with a mix of amusement and focus. Outside, a midsummer rain washed the dust from the patio furniture.

Meg flashed a cheeky salute. "Well done, Julie. What a rowdy bunch this is."

"Indeed," Julie chuckled. "We've got a full docket tonight after Alexi crushed it with Lenny a few weeks ago. Vince, you're up first."

Vince scanned his notes. "Let's see. Since Alexi's radio interview, we've seen a surge in website activity."

Julie, her impatience legendary, pressed forward. "Details?"

He nodded. "Top queries are about where to learn meditation, followed closely by where to attend meetings. We need to clarify these on our site. There's also interest in Alexi traveling to other cities for meetings and private counseling. My personal favorite—'Can I bring my dog?' Ellie's doing a fantastic job maintaining the website, but it needs an upgrade, and we have to find ways to lighten her workload—just my opinion."

Soon after Ellie joined what would become known as *The Meetings*, it became clear she was the glue holding everything together—and as they soon realized, a lot of glue was needed.

Vince moved through the rest of the agenda before flipping to the last page. "Oh, ya. *Who Am I?* sold out again. We need to decide how many copies to print. All points open for discussion are listed on the handout." He set his notes down and exhaled. "Can I breathe now?"

A shared sense of accomplishment filled the air, reflecting the success of birthing an organization that became a beacon for truth-seekers in St. Cloud—and beyond. After months of no meetings due to COVID, Ellie started hosting Zoom meetings for Alexi, and to everyone's surprise, attendance doubled, then tripled. Still, everyone agreed that nothing compared to being in the same room and sharing that collective energy.

As the discussion chugged on, Alexi gradually tuned out, the chatter fading into the background.

What a little monster I've created, she mused. *I should be doing more, but what about my other projects? I'm coaching the middle school girls' softball team, preparing for two more book signings, and training for the summer bike races. Even though I'm no longer full-time, two days a week as a sub feels like a marathon.*

Her thoughts drifted in scattered fragments as her gaze landed on Ellie, busy taking notes. *Ellie is our savior. What would we do without her? Sofia laughed when I told her about what was happening in St. Cloud. She said she wasn't surprised and said I must have the Great Spirit working overtime. I love that woman.*

"What do you think, Alexi?" Julie's voice cut through Alexi's reverie.

Alexi refocused. "Seems there's a lot on the table. Which point are you referring to?"

Julie recognized the familiar cue, smiled, and recapped. "Some of us think we should commit to a year-long lease on the building we've been renting these past two months. Now that COVID restrictions are lifted, people can't wait to become human again. And kudos to Steve for hosting our meetings for the last five years."

She stood and applauded as others followed her lead. Steve nodded, clearly moved.

Julie turned back to Alexi. "Then there's the whole 'to charge or not to charge' dilemma, or stick with donations?"

"I have an answer for both," Alexi said. "Mom and I checked with Charlie's lawyer last week. He finally confirmed it's a go. Once the papers are signed, my foundation will cover the rental fees for our meetings."

"Julie relaxed back into her chair. "I, too, am starting to love Charlie."

After another half-hour of brainstorming, the meeting wound down, flowing naturally into the usual potluck dinner and social time.

When the last of the group left, Alexi plopped on the couch, cradling her third cup of tea. A contented smile lingered as she reminisced about the evening's conversations. *I'm happy with the informal meetings and glad we organized the weekend bike trip on the Mesabi Trail—something I've always wanted to do.*

Her thoughts shifted to the potluck dishes: Vince's overambitious lasagna, Ellie's salad, as meticulous as her planning, and Julie's daring dessert. Each dish, a testament to the heart and dedication everyone brought to the group.

Yet, the 'real' world pulled her back to an ever-present to-do list that never quite seemed to end. Her Little Red Pony—her beloved car—was sitting in the driveway, waiting patiently for an oil change.

Her thoughts pivoted to planning the grocery list for

Sunday dinner. The thought of that weekly ritual with Lyam and her mom warmed her. She smiled, recalling the day Lyam took her and her mom for a balloon ride. *What a day that was. Sometimes, I wonder if I was born under a lucky star.*

Chapter 39

Scissors Meditation

The weekly meeting began as usual—small talk about the weather, weekend plans, the familiar hum of conversation as people milled about the room. Once everyone was seated, Bob opened the discussion. "I read the section about forgiveness on your site, and honestly, I find it difficult to practice."

"I get it," Alexi responded. "I've been there. Let me share something that happened to me. When I moved out of my first apartment, the landlord kept $200 of my deposit even though her manager said everything looked great. I was livid. You might have been through something similar—maybe not a money thing—possibly a betrayal in a relationship or being wronged somehow. As I held on to my anger, it impacted both my body and mental well-being. The effects of blame extend far and wide."

Alexi paused, gauging the effects of her story, then continued, "Lyam was a big help here. He asked me how much mental space my anger and desire for revenge occupied. Even when I followed his advice and acknowledged the unreality of blame, I couldn't let it go. Then he gave me the most unexpected advice. Want to know the curveball he threw at me?"

Everyone gave Alexi a go-ahead nod. "He told me to get a

pair of scissors and cut it out of my life."

A puzzled silence fell over the room, followed by a few hesitant laughs.

"Yeah, I know," Alexi said. That was my reaction too. I thought he was joking—but not. He led me through an exercise that worked famously for me. He called it the *Scissors Meditation*. How about we all close our eyes, and let's give it a go, shall we?"

The group settled into their seats, and Alexi began. "First, get comfortable and release today's tension. Raise your shoulders, then let them drop. Roll your head gently and relax your neck. Take a minute to scan each part of your body from head to toe."

After a pause, she continued, "Feel your body where it meets the chair or floor. Feel the fabric of your clothes, the pulse of your heartbeat. Relax and let go. There's nothing you need to do now except follow a few simple instructions. I will give you plenty of time for this exercise.

"Let's start by thinking of someone you hold a grudge against, possibly someone who mistreated you or caused you pain. It may be someone you hate or only mildly dislike. Pick only one person. As you bring them to mind, notice any physical discomfort or tightness in your body. Where do you feel it? Allow your attention to go to the area that feels tense or ill at ease. If you start condemning, blaming, or replaying the story, you're thinking, not sensing. Bring your attention back to the body, to the area that feels off in the chest or stomach area. If you're telling yourself, 'I'm over this person, I've forgiven them,' but you've chosen them for this exercise, odds are there's still something lingering inside."

After letting everyone settle into this exercise for a few minutes, Alexi continued, "You must be a good detective with this endeavor. Sometimes, the clues are obvious; at other times, your ego may try to distract you with diversions and denials.

Allow your attention to be with any discomfort that arises. Let your body take the lead. It's a matter of sensing, not analyzing. Ask what's at the heart of this.

"Try to connect those uneasy feelings with the person you've chosen. Notice any images, colors, or sensations that arise as you explore your inner landscape. Give these images your attention. See if the unease carries a quality you can match with feeling words or images that capture its essence. Try some to see which is the best fit. Be careful not to let your mind take charge and start replaying the story around this person. Sense any sadness, or irritation, or whatever in your chest or stomach. Take your time; there's no rush. Unravel this at your own pace."

Alexi glanced around the room, aware she was guiding most into unfamiliar territory, but pressed on. "Now, picture a cord connecting you to that person. It may originate from your chest or stomach, where you feel tension or discomfort. This isn't fantasy. A physical cord attaches us to everyone we have contact with. It can be subtle and ethereal or a heavy cord of blame. Take a moment to visualize the cord extending from that place of distress within you to the other person."

She paused, letting the image settle.

"Now, in your mind's eye, imagine a pair of mystic scissors of any size or shape. When you're ready, use them to cut the cord. Continue to cut until you feel the connection is entirely severed and you are both floating free. Allow yourself some time for this process."

Alexi scanned the room. Some brows were knitted in concentration at the enormity of the task. Others looked serene, as though one more gentle snip was all that was needed. She gave the group a little more time and encouragement.

"Good. When finished, put your scissors away and take some moments to reflect. Do you see this person differently now? You may feel neutral, or maybe a warmth has replaced old tensions.

You may feel like smiling and giving them a hug. Or there could still be a twinge of 'hmm, something's still not right.'

Ellie, please ring the bell in a few minutes so we can discuss our experiences."

When the bell chimed, Loni was eager to report. "That was incredible! I picked my former husband, thinking things were fine between us, and he would be an easy choice. But I realized there's more under the surface than I'd admitted. I guess I've been avoiding examining our relationship, trying to act 'spiritual' about, well, our entire marriage."

Alexi nodded understandingly and held her gaze before turning to Jerry." Jerry, anything you'd like to say?"

"How did you know?" Jerry asked, amazed that she'd zeroed in on him. "For me, it was someone I hated. Bill and I were business partners until he betrayed me and joined our competitors. That hurt, and I spent years despising him. Want the details?"

"Absolutely."

"Okay," Jerry took a deep breath. "I resisted the exercise at first because it sounded kind of goofy. Then Bill came to mind, and I resisted even more, thinking he didn't deserve my forgiveness. Still, I gave it a shot, though I wasn't hopeful."

He exhaled and took another breath. "During the exercise, I remembered a line I once read: 'When we blame, we think we're on the side of God, but God doesn't take sides.' That hit hard. I realized I'd been using God as an excuse to justify my anger, as if I were working with God because Bill needed to be punished. Then, in an instant, I realized how ridiculous that was—I was only hurting myself.

"With that, I couldn't wait to pull out this enormous pair of scissors and start cutting away. The cord was tenacious, but I was determined. It was amazing. As I hacked away, I felt this massive release, like something inside physically snapped, as if this heavy, dark weight in my stomach—well, it just let go. I started to laugh as I noticed how free I felt, and then I began to breathe—I mean, really breathe. As you can see, I am still trying to catch my breath."

Jerry's voice trembled, "I realized this cord of blame no longer connected us, and by releasing him, I was releasing myself. I waved, wished him well, and watched him fly away on little angel wings. And now," he paused, "I don't know why these tears are flowing."

"Hmm, I wonder!" Alexi nodded with a smile.

"Thank you. Thank you. Thank you." Jerry whispered with hand on heart.

"This is a good note to end on. We'll delve more into this exercise during our upcoming weekend retreat. Sometimes, once isn't enough. These cords are like vines that can sometimes grow back—sometimes not."

Chapter 40

Forgiveness

In the calm aftermath of the previous Friday's meditation, Barb, a regular at the meetings, was eager to share: "Big shoutout to Jerry for sharing last week. His story made me rethink my half-hearted attempt with the scissors meditation last week, but forgiving my mom? Forget it. I constantly get stuck with her. 'Why is she so critical?' 'I wish she were more, blah, blah, blah.' I know how important forgiveness is for my mental well-being, so after hearing Jerry's report, I gave it a shot at home and noticed an improvement with how I saw my mom."

Alexi's eyes brightened, "That's fantastic to hear! Lyam once shared a bit of wisdom with me—he said we spend countless hours mastering the art of judging and holding grudges, but if we freed that energy, we'd uncover an inner quiet that whispers what truly matters in life. When we cut the cord, their hold over us vanishes—love flows, and both sides win. Even though we cut the cord of discord, a faint, harmonious thread remains on a subtle level."

Barb nodded, and Alexi continued, "Lyam's scissors meditation was a game-changer for me. I practiced it for an entire week on one of my retreats, and it completely transformed how

I relate with people. As a kid, my mom often said, 'Just cut it out.' That's exactly what I did with my imaginary scissors."

"Hmm," Barb mused. "My mom also says that. Would you say you've completely moved past resenting others?"

Alexi thought for a moment. "I can't remember the last time I held a grudge. And the small stuff? I cut loose as soon as possible. But it wasn't easy. At times, I felt it insurmountable. Letting go of the baggage of old regrets and grudges felt like coming face-to-face with a bear in the woods—my instinct was to turn and run. I no longer wanted to be a puppet in the hands of others. I asked for grace and found the courage to persist."

"Interesting!" Barb commented. "I don't know if I will—or even want to—reach that point with my ex."

"I get it," Alexi replied. "It's not an easy meditation. When I was in middle school, my volleyball coach seemed to specialize in criticism—never a word of praise. When I spoke to Lyam about her he called it a CBE—a Character Building Exercise—and compared my resentment to an ocean wave."

Alexi smiled, recalling Lyam's insights from years before. "He told me to see my thoughts, feelings, and grudges as waves in the ocean. Whether stormy or gentle, what do all waves have in common?"

"Water," Barb answered.

"Exactly," Alexi replied. "No matter the nature of the wave, it's all the same ocean. And like a wave, your thoughts rise, exist for a moment, and then merge into the vast ocean of Being. The ego's need for self-importance fuels blame— 'I've been wronged.' With that mindset, looking through the ego's lens, we'll always find something to grumble about."

Alexi's mind drifted back to her college days when Lyam wasn't just her cycling coach, he was her life coach. He'd often revisit the wave analogy, adding new insights to keep it fresh and relevant.

Drawing on Lyam's wisdom, she continued, "If we viewed our thoughts as waves in the ocean, judgments and blame would dissolve like salt in water. We'd learn to ride out rogue waves without taking them so seriously. Can a wave be judged imperfect? Can a wave be separate from the ocean? No. We are the boundless ocean, simply taking the form of a wave."

Always mindful not to monopolize the discussion, Barb let out a resounding "Phew" and signed off with heartfelt thanks.

Sonia was eager to pick up the thread, "I get what you're saying, and it makes sense, but when I tried to forgive my ex-girlfriend, it felt like I was swimming in a pool of forgotten laundry."

"You feel she doesn't deserve forgiveness?" Alexi nudged her on.

"Absolutely," Sonia's voice was firm. "What she did was unforgivable and immoral—and it wasn't the first time she trashed me."

Alexi nodded, "I hear you. No one should feel obligated to forgive something immoral, and no one should expect to be forgiven for wrongdoing. But here's a twist—what if we saw every action as innocent as an ocean wave? Think about it. Can we call a scorpion's sting or a lion hunting a gazelle evil, or even a mistake? There are cells in our bodies we label 'harmful,' but they're just doing what they're meant to do. From their perspective, white blood cells—like Arlo and Zoe—are the real intruders."

Alexi paused. "The challenge with forgiveness isn't about excusing bad behavior but questioning whether our concepts of good and bad are truly valid. Forgiveness isn't glossing over wrongdoings or pretending nothing happened. It's recognizing there's nothing inherently wrong to forgive."

"So, I should let her walk all over me?" Sonia's voice was tight with frustration.

"Forgiveness isn't about condoning violence and injustice or failing to intervene in harmful behavior. It's realizing that our true battle is with our misconceptions about good and evil."

"I'm lost," Sonia responded quickly. "One minute, you're talking about forgiveness. Now you're saying there's nothing to forgive. So, what's the scissors meditation about?"

Alexi acknowledged the conundrum at the heart of forgiveness. *It would be easier if the world were clear-cut and logical—neatly packaged into right and wrong—making my job a lot easier.* She took a deep breath and pressed on.

"On one hand, forgiveness is impossible because every action is a reflection of Absolute Being. Yet, here we are, living in a world of contradictions. Imagine our world as a masterpiece of incredible beauty yet marred by smudges and flaws. These blemishes are part of the bigger picture, where beauty and imperfection coexist—perfectly imperfect. So, when we talk about forgiveness, we face a paradox—how can forgiveness be relevant where mistakes are as insignificant as the rise and fall of an ocean wave? The scissors meditation, combined with a deeper understanding of forgiveness, helps us avoid getting stuck in a quagmire of blame and regret, allowing our energy to flow freely."

She paused, letting the words settle. "The scissors meditation isn't about correcting wrongs or affirming what's right, it's about seeing beyond both. And what's found there? Love—a profound love that's the destination of forgiveness."

"So, is forgiveness a path to awakening?" Sonia asked.

"No," Alexi hesitated for a moment. "Yes."

"Glad we cleared that up!"

Alexi smiled and shifted gears. "Let's talk about the art of living. When we realize that our actions—and those of others—are as fleeting and trivial as an ocean wave, the need for forgiveness dissolves into the vastness of the sea. Until that time, the scissors meditation serves to free us from those who are like anchors, dragging us to the bottom of the ocean. Just like a car can't run smoothly with a clogged air filter, clearing our judgments helps liberate ourselves, allowing us to pursue the ultimate goal, awakening to your true self."

"Whew!" Sonia exhaled as if she'd just finished a marathon.

"I second that 'Whew,'" Alexi smiled. "Contentment lies in seeing through the facade of others' deeds, so there's no need for forgiveness. Yet, forgiveness becomes inevitable in this unfolding masterpiece we call life."

"That's a lot to wrap my head around," Sonia muttered.

"I hear you," Alexi nodded. "When Lyam first spoke to me about forgiveness, I couldn't make sense of it either. My mom told me Lyam's book was a metaphor for life. These meetings are like that—a way to make sense of a world that will always remain elusive. On the surface, our talks might seem pointless, even absurd. But once we embrace this dreamlife, with forgiveness, I guarantee that the light of love will shine through your eyes. Forgive and have sweet dreams. That's what this forgiveness is about."

Chapter 41

Picnic in the Park

It was one of those perfect sunny days in St. Cloud. Beneath the sprawling branches of maple trees in Riverside Park, Mira and Alexi were transforming a picnic table into a festive spread. Lyam pulled up in his pickup truck and stepped out with a bag of charcoal and a cooler. Inside the cooler: a pound of fresh hamburger, a six-pack of Coors Light, and a jar of lemonade.

Alexi looked into the cooler, a smile lighting her face. It was September 5th, her thirty-first birthday, and all three were flexitarians when the occasion called.

"Lyam, good to see you with the contraband!" she giggled.

"I can't remember the last time, if ever, I bought beer and hamburglar," he chuckled, his malapropism adding charm to the occasion.

As Lyam flipped the burgers, Mira arranged the table. Baked beans, potato salad, and condiments, all served on a red-and-white checkered tablecloth completed the classic Midwestern spread.

They ate, they talked, they cleaned up, and soon, their feet fell into rhythm with the Mississippi River. As they walked, they congratulated themselves for finally coming together to discuss Alice's manuscript.

Once they returned, Alexi and Lyam opened a can of beer while Mira opted for a glass of lemonade. Alexi flipped open her laptop. "I'm glad we're doing this because I'm curious to hear if you think her writing is worthy of a book. It took me forever to sift through her cross-outs and arrows."

She scrolled through her notes, bracing for what promised to be a long afternoon. "Okay, let's start here: Alice mentions she left the rez in the fall of '59, about two and a half years after first arriving, but doesn't go into much detail about the why."

"I can tell you," Lyam said. "I was around sixteen and shocked when I heard her asking for a ride heading west. She seemed happy at the rez but eventually confessed to Sofia and me that her destiny was to live in San Francisco. She called it the axis the world revolves around."

Alexi's fingers raced to capture every word. "Interesting! When she returned to the rez three years later for her vision quest, does she talk about her part in 'turning the world?'" she asked with a touch of sarcasm.

"She did," Lyam said. "She described San Francisco as a mecca for spiritual renewal and felt part of that movement. When she returned, I was nineteen and happy to see her again. She said she only came to do a vision quest. Well, you know what happened then."

"We sure do," Alexi grinned as she scrolled down the page. "Her journal picks up when she's back in San Francisco after leaving Mira with you at the rez. I cherry-picked my favorites to give you a taste, but her book reads like a who's-who of the '60s and '70s. Here are Alice's words:

Far out, man. No more stuck in a convent at the rez. I've made the cosmic leap back, and the vibe is electrifying. Leo's still running the show at the Coffee Gallery and is over the moon to see me again. Instead of tossing me back into my old waitress gig serving up joe, he lays this on me, 'You gonna be my manager now!' That threw me for a loop 'cause I was raking in serious bread on tips. But Leo says this gig's about booking speakers and bands. I'm all in on that one.

"Whenever we moved," Mira reminisced, her voice radiating admiration, "she'd land a waitressing job. I was amazed at her schmoozing skills. She encouraged me, but I wasn't cut out for that kind of thing."

Alexi scrolled to another page. "Alice wrote almost daily for that first year. Mostly about the people she met and the bands and speakers she booked. I could practically feel the excitement in her words. One entry I found fascinating was her interaction with Grace Slick. She says she booked The Great Society band not long after she got back. Here's how she describes that night:

October '65, man, that's the date the big 'U' carved this stellar crossroads for Grace and me. It was her first gig, but her vibe was unreal. She opened my mind to the power of music. A night filled with peace and love sent us floating on a sea of endless possibilities.

"She writes more about Grace's presence at the Coffee Gallery and how grateful Grace was for the opportunity."

"I do know they were friends," Mira added. "Remember when I told you that I babysat for her daughter, China, when I was a teen?"

Alexi took a reluctant breath before continuing, "Here Alice expressed her disappointment over missing Janis Joplin's performance at the Coffee Gallery because she was at the rez having a baby. Reading that made me tear up."

Mira's voice dropped. "I always felt I was an imposition in her life,"

"That's hard for me to hear too," Lyam admitted. "That was a sore spot for us. She wanted to be the kind of mother she never had, but she didn't have the tools to make that happen. I knew she wasn't happy after Mira was born, so I offhandedly suggested she return to San Francisco. But when she did just that, I was shocked. I never dreamed she would leave Mira at the rez. And when she came back almost four years later and took Mira…" His voice trailed off as he twirled a fallen leaf between his fingers.

After an emotional pause, Alexi continued, "I hadn't tuned into Grace's song *White Rabbit* until I read what Alice wrote, and then I must have listened to it countless times. It's beautiful, haunting, and epitomizes the '60s. Here's Alice:

Leo's da man. Let's me do my thing, so I'm at the Matrix when the Great Society grooves, laying down tracks before the Jefferson Airplane takes flight. Watching Grace is a pure high. And when the tribe needs wisdom, there's this cosmic chant, Ask Alice. I think she'll know.' My life: drugs, rock, and living on the edge.

"Alice writes that a few months later, Grace was *floating in another realm* when she penned *White Rabbit*."

"Do you think what Alice says is true?" Lyam asked pensively.

"I do. I can tell by her notes. Her job took a lot of organization, so she used notebooks as a things-to-do list, doubling as a diary."

"But enough of Grace. I may have fallen down a rabbit hole," Alexi chuckled. "And get this: in February of '66, Ronald, your wanna-be dad, and Alice drive to LA for a music fest. There, Alice sees a poster advertising the *Watts Acid Test*. It's the first-ever massive acid rock party with Kool-Aid-laced LSD and took place six months after the Watts Riots. Alice called it the dawn of the hippie era. She writes pages about it, which I found fascinating and educational. The only band I recognized from that evening's lineup was *The Grateful Dead*."

"Whew!" Mira exhaled, turning to Lyam. "You were Alice's age. How did the wildness affect you?"

"It didn't. Life on the rez and my monk days at Tassajara were worlds apart from Alice's scene. I played catch-up when I moved to Crestone. But this is Alice's time, and her diary helps me understand her better."

Mira interjected, "I think Alice wanted to belong, and those mercurial rock bands were a perfect fit—she could belong and not at the same time." Mira paused and took a deep breath. "This is heavy stuff for me. Maybe we should go for another stroll so I can reboot?"

When they returned, Alexi restarted her laptop and dug back in. "School never taught me half as much about the anti-war movement as reading Alice. In 1971, Alice and Mom traveled east and dove into anti-war demonstrations. She devotes nine pages to the April 1971 protest in DC alone.

"Oh, yes," Mira said, "that's when someone took a picture of Alice and me when I was eight, the one on our fridge. Alice tied a stretchy band to our wrists so I wouldn't get lost. At some point, everything turned chaotic. I remember my eyes burning from tear gas and crying when I saw police clobbering people with batons and dragging them down the street." Mira shivered. "It was my wake-up to life's grim realities. Mom left me with a friend the next day when she returned to the protest. I was terrified that night when she didn't come home."

After a pause, Alexi continued, "I thought Alice did a great job capturing the intensity. She says it was the biggest anti-war protest ever. They wanted to shut down Washington, especially the Justice Department, using their bodies as blockades. She says it was mostly peaceful, yet 12,000 people were arrested. Alice writes that she was happy and proud to be among them. She was placed behind a makeshift wire fence, the same one where the famous anti-war activist Dr. Spock was held. They were then transported to the Washington Colosseum and given blankets for the night. The next day, the police didn't know what to do with them, so they let most go."

Mira exhaled a slow 'whew.' Feeling this again in a new light felt odd. "I get it now. I understand how vital those protests were, and I, too, am proud of Mom. Those demonstrations helped end the war. She lived her dream of being an agent of change."

Alexi continued, "I was skeptical when I first read that Alice wanted to help reshape the world. But she did. Her perspective on the government and the hippie mindset opened my eyes. She says our government was in a fog—arrogance, she calls it—dismissing the counter-culture movement as drug-crazed kids. She says drugs gave her the gift of clarity, helping her see through the war propaganda. Alice was a mover and shaker, and it saddens me to think I never knew that side of her."

The sun started to set across the river, adding to the surreal atmosphere. Alexi looked up and asked, "Are you guys okay with one more segment I found fascinating?"

"Absolutely," Mira agreed as Lyam nodded.

"Alice seemed to have a fascination with John Lennon and often talked about wanting to meet him. In December 1971, he performed a benefit concert in Ann Arbor for John Sinclair, who was serving ten years for a minor drug offense. Alice knew one of the groups playing with Lennon and managed to get invited backstage, where she briefly met him. It may be a coincidence, but three days later, Sinclair was freed."

Alexi paused and took a deep breath. "I got emotional reading her account of the day John Lennon was killed in 1980. She says she was in New York, meeting with Charlie's lawyers to set up a fund for Mira, who was about to turn eighteen. Let me read what she says because I found it poetic and touching."

For most in NYC, it was a cold but beautiful December day. For me, it was the day the music truly died. The world I dug ceased to exist. I took the packed subway to Central Park for his vigil, where over 100,000 of us were crammed together. Yet I felt alone, no longer having a purpose or will to live.

At 2 p.m., we observed a ten-minutes of silence to honor John. Silence always freaked me out, like a bad trip I wanted to escape from. But I was trapped, surrounded by a mass of grieving souls. The crowd magnified the silence, and I slipped into a stillness I had never known. At first, I felt only the warmth of John's loving presence. But as I stood there, my past traumas began flashing their ghoulish faces, taunting me. I was terrified and promised myself never again to allow my ghosts to resurface and pollute the world or Mira.

As Alexi finished, a warm pink glow was visible across the river. Mira pulled a sheet from the roll of paper towels on the table, blew her nose, and wiped her eyes. Lyam put his arm around Mira as Alexi closed her laptop.

Lost for words, Mira quietly said, "Let's go home."

They packed their belongings into their vehicles and drove off into the twilight like a troupe of wandering troubadours. A waning crescent moon lingered in the western sky, a silent witness to the story of a wounded traveler who struggled to navigate the treacherous currents of a life-stream.

Chapter 42

Love

As the autumn sun set, it cast a warm glow over the cozy meeting room. Soft, eggshell-colored walls enclosed a casual mix of cushions and chairs, creating an inviting yet simple space. Jill's voice gently broke the silence once the group's meditation ended.

"I feel a profound stillness during my recent meditations, especially tonight. I know you mentioned true love is beyond feeling, but it sure feels like love."

A quiet settled over the room until a hand was raised. Alexi spoke softly, "Would it be all right if we hold other questions tonight and only talk about love?"

Murmurs of agreement rippled through the room. Alexi picked up a paper from her side table.

"I was going to discuss this question tonight: 'What is the purpose of my life?'" she paused, holding up the paper. "I don't know how I would answer that. Maybe I'd say life has no purpose. But that wouldn't be entirely correct. Life's purpose is Love. "If there's a one-word answer to Lyam's book title, *Who Am I?*, it's love. Love is that aspect of Absolute Being that radiates peace, happiness, and a deep joy." Alexi glanced at Jill. "Love is beyond the realm of feeling. To glimpse love reveals love's meaning."

Jill and Alexi first met at Steve's apartment, where their friendship took root. Jill and Steve, both passionate social workers, started their Friday evening spiritual discussion group a year before Alexi joined. For them, these gatherings were a welcome relief to connect with like-minded people.

"You say it's not that deep feeling I have inside, yet you say love can be glimpsed. I don't get it?" Jill asked.

"Love is unconditional, transcending feelings and glimpses," Alexi continued. "Yet, feelings of love arise from the core of our Being. While it's impossible to feel or glimpse love directly, its radiance can illuminate our perceptions, casting a warm glow on the world we perceive. Lyam calls this 'the interface between absolute reality and our relative existence.'"

Alexi's gaze shifted from some faraway thought and settled back on the group. "I love talking about love. Did that help, Jill?"

Jill nodded. A pause lingered before Marv spoke. "I've never experienced what Jill has. I can't help being a bit envious."

Alexi's smile mirrored her understanding. "I know what you mean. It was also that way for me."

"Really? Would you feel comfortable talking about that?" Marv was quick to ask.

"Hmm…" Alexi tilted her head. "That's an interesting ask. I've never shared my personal experience of love in a group meeting before. But yes, I would 'love' to," she smiled.

"Encounters with love always fascinate me. In Lyam's book, he hints at the intangible nature of love through Arlo's first kiss with Zoe. I read that part dozens of times, and at fourteen, I knew that's what I wanted. I always assumed it would happen with a romantic partner, so I was caught off guard when I discovered it at a humble Indian ashram."

Alexi gathered her thoughts before diving into the story of her pilgrimage.

"My first trip East was to a Buddhist center in Sri Lanka, recommended by Lyam. There, I met someone who told stories of an Indian ashram he'd visited. After the retreat, I headed to India. That decision was a game-changer for me. I found myself knee-deep in a reality opposite to my life in Minnesota or anything I experienced at Buddhist retreats. I'm still somewhat dumbfounded, but something profound happened to the former Alexi there.

"It could've been the chanting, the bowing, the meditations, the incense, the pujas, or just the guru's presence, but my heart cracked open. It felt like a direct hit from Cupid's arrow. My mind stopped its chatter, and tears—oh blessed tears—began to flow for days. These were tears of purification, washing away layers of deep-seated pain, leaving me with uncontained joy. I spent four months at that ashram, sharing a humble dorm with three other women. Despite the challenges of living in India, I valued my time there more than a vacation on a yacht in the Mediterranean."

Alexi glanced around the room, catching curious eyes and feeling their silent encouragement. "As I floated through this surreal experience, the familiar boundaries of reality began to blur. It felt like I was being rewired, as if my circuit board was being upgraded to handle more powerful energy. At the time, I knew I was in love, but the question was, with whom? The guru? Absolutely. The ashram's mystical aura? Without a doubt. But my bliss didn't end there. It extended to my roommates and whatever else came to my awareness, including my grandmother, Alice."

She paused, then added, "Later, when I shared my experience with Lyam, he said that when the heart flows, it recognizes no boundaries or limitations. He said that when we break free from the chains of our hopes and dreams, all that's left is pure, unconditional love."

"Wow!" Marv exhaled, "It feels like I've been missing

something. I thought these meetings were about gaining a new perspective on life. Now I hear you talking about love, and that's something I'll never..."

Alexi gazed at Marv empathically. She sensed the weight of the conversation, and her voice lightened with a graceful switch of gears. "Here's the deal with our Friday night specials. Part one: We tackle what Lyam calls 'the facts of life.' That's like lifting the curtain to see what's going on backstage. Lyam insists that the mind needs its fair share of clarity.

"And part two? Well, that's the heart of the matter, literally. It's what Jill was talking about, the finest feeling level. But this isn't a skill that can be picked up like a sport. It's more like an energy or vibe you catch from a book, a group, or your favorite spiritual Yoda."

The room fell silent until Jill finally spoke. "Thanks. I'm blown away. But this love thing isn't all rainbows and butterflies for me. It's hard to put into words. It's not exactly pain, but, oh, I don't know."

"I totally relate," Alexi said softly. "Love has a way of expressing itself in unique ways. For me, love manifests as a flow of tears and a sinking into an ocean of peace and joy. But underneath this calm, there's an ache—a craving for a purer love, just out of reach. It's a lover's dilemma, a marriage that can never be consummated, no matter how heart-wrenching the desire, yet a rapture that melts the heart to oblivion. I call it an *aching intimacy*, and sometimes, *sweet sadness*."

Alexi closed her eyes and looked inward. "Even though pure love can't be fully experienced, it's merciful and beckons me to advance only so far, lest I get consumed and am no longer an instrument in its service. Possibly, it's what a moth feels as it circles the flame, throbbing for a single touch of the flame's ecstatic beauty. As I search my mind for the cause, I find only invisible, ineffable bliss.

She paused thoughtfully. “Literature is filled with stories of *sweet sadness*. The drama of our lives is a constant dance between the heart and mind, love and fear. Despite our efforts to describe love, we can only talk about what love is like. Yet love isn’t a simile; love can only be itself.”

Alexi closed her eyes for a few minutes, relishing the silence. “I think it’s time for tea.”

Chapter 43

Sally Gets It

"Welcome, everyone!" Alexi greeted the evening's participants, picking up her notebook from the side table with a playful smile. "Someone mentioned that I tend to elaborate too much when answering questions. So tonight, I'm aiming to be more judicious. Let's see how I do with this eclectic mix."

What is the purpose of life?
"Why insist on a purpose? The pursuit of some grand meaning keeps us looking for the next experience, as if fulfillment lies somewhere beyond the present. This endless search, driven by the ego's craving for different and better, can obscure the simple flow of life. Real peace and love arise when we embrace the moment, and in that surrender, deeper truths naturally emerge, revealing our worldly purpose without expectation."

I assume you no longer have an ego. How can I eliminate mine?
"I do have an ego, but it's no longer the captain of my ship. The ego isn't inherently negative, but a helpful tool that arises in the form of thoughts to assist me in navigating life. As long as the body exists, some traces of an ego will remain. The aim isn't to

eliminate the ego, but to realize that isn't who you truly are.

"If there are two captains, there will be conflict. As the individual ego, nurtured by self-awareness, rises to the status of the cosmic ego—your true self, it takes a backseat, and at some point, is seen not to exist. The struggle between 'two' dissolves, and what remains is a life lived in harmony and love."

What's your view about death, heaven, hell, reincarnation, and past lives?

"Whew! That's a biggie," Alexi grinned, playfully swiping a hand across her brow. "For sure, the body dies. But at our meetings, we explore what remains untouched by death—the eternal, unchanging self—the ocean, not the waves. Death only shatters our reflection in the mirror, not our true nature. There's an initial sting as the body's essence dissolves into the ether, yet this can happen with the awareness that the body never was and Being never was not.

"Yes, there's a heaven. It's a place of light in the cosmic afterlife. Hell lurks in the shadows where barriers of fear and ignorance block the light. Both realms are customized to each person's unique tendencies. Nothing is permanent. The dark clouds will eventually fade, and the light of Being will shine through.

"Death shouldn't be foreign to us. We slip into a small death each night, only to emerge reincarnated into a fresh version of ourselves. At death, the body's elements and subtle energies return to the elements. This process, recycling into new forms, can spark intuitions of past lives. And hey, maybe our chances of returning after the 'big sleep' hinge on how entertaining we've been."

Alexi chuckled, enjoying the economy of her answers. "I aim to exit with no unfinished business, no regrets, no grudges. I let death be my life coach. By finding humor in all I do, I hope to go out with a smile."

Can you explain what you mean by nonduality and why you say our world is not real? If I hit my head on a wall, it sure feels real.

"In our meetings, we explore many topics, but when we touch on the ultimate nature of existence, I speak in terms of nonduality. Nonduality means "not two"—one consciousness, one reality, expressing itself as everything. We and the world are reflections of a single Absolute Reality. It's like gold jewelry appearing in different forms, yet still only gold.

"Dualism, on the other hand, assumes fundamental divisions: God and creation, good and evil, me and others. It sees God or Absolute Reality as distinct from us and the world.

"If you hit your head on a wall, it hurts—but once the pain fades, it becomes just another passing moment in the unfolding drama of your life. What comes and goes is like a dream—real in experience, yet unreal at its core. Beneath it all is unchanging, ever-present consciousness that is the source of everything. In this light, life reveals itself as both real and unreal, both dual and non-dual.

"I emphasize the 'unreal' aspect because we've been conditioned since childhood to see the world as solid and unquestionably real, never recognizing its dreamlike, illusory nature. Our meetings offer another perspective, where the world is seen to be as insubstantial as a mirage in the desert. When we begin to see through the mental constructs we've taken for granted, something shifts—life becomes lighter, less burdensome.

"This perspective isn't about rejecting the world, but living with ease, knowing you're not separate from Absolute Reality. It's the belief that we are separate from the Source that gives rise to suffering. My advice to you is to wake up and realize you're not just *in* the universe, but *are* the universe, playing out your unique role in the form of a person."

I found the part about human-helpers in your book interesting. Do you believe they're intelligent and consciously helping us?
"I'm surprised many don't believe this. Cells exhibit not only individual intelligence but also collective wisdom. The same goes for organs—like the liver or heart—and for flocks of birds or schools of fish.

"Human-helpers are undoubtedly intelligent. Evolution begins at the cellular level, where countless cells cooperate to create the miracle of the human body. The universe relies on this intricate web of collaboration. Beyond our microscopes, entire realms exist—far more complex than we can imagine.

"Galaxies, ecosystems, and atoms display a silent harmony that's a testament to universal intelligence."

Alexi paused and looked up with a half-smile. "The only thing that may not be intelligent… is humans."

She caught a few laughs and set her notebook aside with a pat. "Remember, I did promise to be brief. Anything else tonight?"

Sally started the night's conversation. "Last week, I was driving to work and wondered what it would be like to be in your shoes."

"That's an intriguing thought. But let me turn the tables on you. Ask yourself, what's it like to be Sally?"

"Hmm, let me think," Sally paused. "Well, it's often good, but recently…"

"I mean right now," Alexi interjected. "What's it like to be Sally in this moment?"

Sally exhaled, her voice wavering. "It's scary, you know, sitting here, feeling all eyes on me. I'm lost for words."

"I get it. But try this. Close your eyes and ask yourself, 'What's it like to be Sally right now?'"

"I'm not sure what you want me to do."

"There's no need to understand. It's more of sensing or feeling. What's stirring inside now?"

Alexi paused and scanned the others in the group. "Let's all give it a go. Close your eyes and ask, 'What's it like to be me?' Keep asking yourself this question."

The room became still, as if the air itself joined in.

"If you feel you've reached a resolution, keep probing. Look deeper to finer levels." Alexi's voice was calm, unhurried. "Again, what is this 'me' beyond the labels and characteristics that define you? Who or what is this Sally or Bob beyond sensations or thoughts?"

She paused again, letting the words settle. "Ask yourself what's present now and yesterday, unchanged by your circumstances, emotions, and relationships. What's always there, always here? What remains constant without a name or label?"

Alexi's words flowed slowly. "Consider what's the same about this person now and when you were a child. Investigate—ask what's there that never changes."

Silence stretched until Alexi noticed a shift in Sally's expression. "Sally, I see a smile. What's that about?"

"Oh, Alexi…" Sally's voice trembled with emotions that words couldn't quite express. She gestured, hoping her hands would convey what words could not.

Alexi's smile was warm and knowing. "You've asked many questions in the past, but now you're speechless. Can you tell me what that's about?"

Sally stumbled, her voice barely a whisper. "Words? I can't find any that work."

Alexi leaned forward. "I hear you clearly but try to put a word or label on what's happening inside."

"I can't. There's nothing to say because there's nothing to say about."

Alexi nodded. Every time she heard someone describe this shift, it was unique—yet, somehow, the same. It was fascinating how a certain insight could cut through the mental fog to reveal the essence of one's Being. She remembered her own experience, different in detail but leading to a similar realization. *What a wonder human are*, she mused before continuing.

"After years of searching for Sally, you realize no thoughts or words can capture what it's like to be Sally. And forget the word 'like' because it's not like anything. Now you know the Sally that..."

"Has always been there," Sally finished Alexi's thought. "There's no familiar 'me' anymore. Inside, it feels quiet and empty, like the gap I felt when I lost a tooth as a kid. But at the same time, I—or whatever I am—feel expanded, new." She paused, eyes glancing upward. "Empty—yet full."

Sally's face brightened. "Alexi, I have always been this."

"I have always been this," Alexi repeated. "These are the five most beautiful words ever spoken."

"That's who I am," Sally's voice carried both wonder and disbelief. "Being Sally is nothing like I imagined. It's like I'm talking, but not the Sally I used to believe I was. I never believed people when they said it was a joke, but now I see it is. The funniest part is that it took me so long to see this."

"Is there any confusion?"

"No, for the first time, there's no confusion." Sally closed her eyes before continuing, "There's absolutely no doubt."

Alexi and the group sat silently, each taking in the stillness. Most had their eyes closed, absorbing the moment. After a few minutes, Alexi broke the silence.

"Sally's words aren't ancient phrases from millennium-old scriptures. They're vibrant truths that are alive and relevant today. Maybe it's best if we don't get into anything more tonight. Let's sit in silence for a while before tea."

Chapter 44

Live Life Like It's Real

"Welcome, everyone," Alexi began this Friday's meeting. "I'd like to share an inspiring email I received last week from someone who wishes to remain anonymous."

She picked up a printout from her lap and read:

Thank you for posting your meetings online. I enjoy them and wanted to share an experience.

I sometimes hesitate to ask someone to dance because rejection stings. After Saturday's dance, I came home feeling dejected—someone I liked had turned me down. I fell into my familiar 'poor me' mindset: Why do I keep going to dances? Maybe I should live like a monk.

I'd read your scissors meditation before but never planned to try it. Still, after nearly twenty years of cycling through the same hurt, something in me snapped. I woke at four a.m., feeling worthless and full of resentment—toward her, toward all women.

Lying there, I asked myself: Do I want to keep blaming her, and myself, or do something about it?

On impulse, I reread the scissors meditation, sat up in bed, and asked, What's hurting? Where is that place inside that hurts? It took enormous effort—and maybe a quiet nudge from my guardian angel. My mind insisted she had attacked me, so I had every right to attack back. I kept replaying old resentments, stuck in a loop.

But I persisted, hoping that if I faced the wound directly, it would lose its power. I eventually noticed a dull ache near my intestines—a 'crappy hurt,' I called it. I began cutting cords, one by one. My mind kept pulling me back into anger, but I stayed with the process. After an hour, something shifted. A major cord snapped loose, and suddenly, I smiled at her image. The resentment was gone—just like that.

What a relief, and like Jerry, I caught my breath as if surfacing from underwater. Then came the yawns—deep, effortless, and incredibly calming. By Sunday, my whole mood had changed. Joy replaced the weight of blame.

And how do I feel about her now? I probably won't ask her to dance again soon. But when I saw her at work Monday, I greeted her with a genuine smile and silently thanked her for helping me bring my shadow to light.

I'm not naive enough to think I won't be hurt again. I know I'm sensitive, and life will keep tossing things my way. But that exercise brought such deep relief that I've started reviewing my past for others I haven't yet forgiven.

Thank you, Alexi. I'll keep using it—until, as you say, I reach a place of instant forgiveness.

Alexi lowered the paper, looked up, and said, "If there's one practice I'd recommend to clear the way for awakening, it's forgiveness."

After a long pause, she asked, "Anything else tonight?"

Jim shifted in his seat before speaking, "I've been revisiting some of your past meetings online, and it sounds like you're saying there's no such thing as good and bad or virtue and vice. Does that still hold true?"

Alexi chuckled softly. "That's still the case."

"Based on that, it sounds like you don't believe in morality.

Do you consider yourself amoral?"

"It's not about labeling myself as moral or immoral," Alexi began. "I lean towards actions most people view as good, so they might peg me as moral. But the whole idea of a rigid code—good versus evil, virtue versus sin—no longer resonates with me."

Jim pressed on, "So, you never do anything others might consider bad or immoral?"

Alexi grinned, "Oh, I'm no stranger to mistakes. But if you're talking about sins against God or humanity, no. I still use common terms like 'good' and 'bad' to describe behavior, but I view those concepts as social constructs, rather than absolute truths. Nothing anyone does is inherently good or bad."

"Are you saying the world doesn't need morals?" Jim probed.

"We've circled this idea before. The world is like a dream that starts fading the moment you wake up. If a group wants to create a code of conduct for right and wrong, so be it. But that doesn't make those rules universal truths. The world's gonna do as it will do."

"Are you saying moral codes are meaningless? What stops you from robbing a bank?" Jim challenged.

"Jail," Alexi responded with a laugh, having answered that question several times before. "Just because something isn't absolute doesn't mean it has no value. Art, language, and laws aren't universal constants, yet they shape our lives in profound ways. Morality is a tool we use to navigate life, live together, and keep societies functioning. It's something humans create, and it evolves."

"But isn't there a correlation between morality and spirituality?" Jim was raised Christian and always saw religion as a guiding light for morality. "Aren't enlightened people naturally moral?"

"That's an interesting question," Alexi replied thoughtfully. "Most believe that enlightenment and morality go hand in hand, and many religions popularize this notion. But the two aren't directly connected. Enlightenment isn't about being morally superior, or what you do, or how you behave. It's about uncovering the truth of who you are—what remains when all searching and questions about morality end."

Alexi hesitated, weighing whether to wade into one of her pet peeves—overzealous morality—but went for it. "From my observations, obsessions with morality breed arrogance, creating divisions between people. Moralists often become the missionaries of countless sorrows, waging a 'righteous war' against the world and themselves."

Jim asked with introspection, "Are you talking about the sin of pride?"

"Pride, yes; sin, no," Alexi clarified.

"Hmm?" Jim reflected before easing into his next question. "I saw a YouTube video about a guy in Brazil who helps homeless kids. That's virtuous, right?"

Alexi nodded thoughtfully. "I'm certainly not anti-virtue because I know that virtue and vice, or humility and pride, are opposite ends of life's spectrum. Picture them as the left and right sides of a log. Walk around it, and suddenly, the sides swap places. What's considered good or bad, virtuous or sinful, depends on culture and circumstances—and, of course, the side of the log you're on," she said with a grin. "They're as inseparable as two sides of a coin or the poles of a magnet. One cannot exist without the other. We can view them as natural expressions of consciousness or battle them like troublesome neighbors. But without opposites, wouldn't everything be sort of—bland?"

Alexi paused. "Still with me, Jim?"

Jim nodded, a touch overwhelmed. "I am, but it's a lot for me to take in. I'll revisit the recording later."

Alexi smiled softly. "The more I imbibe Lyam's wisdom, the more I see the common thread connecting all beings. With that comes the feeling that we are all in this together. Hurting or helping others is hurting or helping ourselves."

Alexi continued, "I'm not encouraging you to act recklessly or irresponsibly. I suggest living as if virtue and vice are real, following society's dictates, while keeping in mind that morality is an intricate illusion. Any more questions besides how to avoid jail?"

Chapter 45

Ellie's Contributions

"Ready to go over my notes?" Ellie asked.

"Let's do it," Alexi responded.

They gathered in Alexi's kitchen, as they did every Friday after the evening meeting. On the stove, the kettle slowly approached a boil. Ellie leaned against the counter, flipping through a yellow notepad filled with scribbles indecipherable to even the most experienced codebreakers.

"Good news first. Fred convinced our building owner to fix that obnoxious noise when the heater kicks on—and to remodel the outdated restrooms."

Alexi's eyes brightened, "I'm so looking forward to that."

The kettle whistled. Alexi poured two cups of tea, and they settled on the couch, Ellie's laptop on the coffee table.

Ellie scanned her notes as she spoke, "Zoom took us to a new level, and now I can barely keep up. I spoke with Fred, and he thinks your recordings should be copyrighted or registered so no one can alter them. And if we include your older ones and the few videos we already have, the website will need a facelift."

Ellie noticed Alexi's attention waning but forged ahead, "Now that Jill's moved to Des Moines, she wants to host meetings using your recordings. She's invited you to a weekend of talks and a book signing."

Alexi hesitated. "Visiting Jill sounds fun—but copyright?" Ellie smiled at Alexi's delayed response, knowing Alexi's aversion to all things legal. "Do we need all this? I'm only a biology teacher."

"That's another thing," Ellie pressed forward, trying to keep Alexi focused on business. "Do you want to continue teaching?"

"I do have to pay the rent. And I love teaching."

Unfazed, Ellie continued, "Fred's confident that by fall, we'll have the funds to pay you a real salary. You'll have more time for retreats and to travel to some of these places for talks and workshops." She slid her laptop toward Alexi, pointing to a spreadsheet with requests as far away as Omaha. "You'd make more than a substitute teacher."

Ellie continued as Alexi scrolled through the list. "Fred still thinks having a YouTube channel for promoting retreats and lectures would be helpful."

"Fred and I've been friends since my first meeting in Steve's living room. He's the reason we've got this whole organization, but…"

"Don't say it," Ellie interrupted before hearing Alexi's objections. "I already told him about your stance on that."

"I've always been wary of most spiritual teachers. It wasn't something I wanted for myself." Alexi glanced at the laptop with a smirk. "And now—here I am. How did this happen?"

Ellie tilted her head with a sly grin. "I'm partially to blame. If I hadn't sent your book and video to Lenny..."

Alexi smiled, "Did I ever properly thank you for that? For everything, actually."

Ellie nodded. "You did. Lenny may have opened the door, but you're the reason people walk through it. You're good at what you do—genuine, with a gift for connecting without fostering blind devotion. Look at these requests. People want more of you."

"Oh, crap!" Alexi sighed. "I don't get it. I'm not doing anything special. I just open my mouth and..."

"And what comes out is exactly what people need to hear. You cut through the noise and get to what matters past the fluff we drown in every day. As for the business side of it? My artist friend can't afford canvases because he refuses to commercialize his work. In the end, everything is a business."

"Even though I love Friday meetings, I have doubts about this whole thing. Do I want to do this in my forties?"

"Fred told me you sometimes sound like his whiny ten-year-old," Ellie grinned.

Alexi laughed. "I guess I do at times."

"Fred also thinks it's time you graduated from coffee table meetings to a real office."

Alexi glanced around the room. "I know, I know, it's got that homey vibe, doesn't it? But it feels more relaxed, less business-y." She caught Ellie's familiar 'it is a business' glance and chuckled. "Okay, point taken. Enough. Another cup of tea?"

Ellie nodded, recognizing the cue. *Enough* means shop's over. She closed her laptop and tucked her notes away.

"I forgot to ask how it feels to finally have your degree?" Alexi asked.

"Pretty darn good," Ellie exhaled. "I'm glad I settled on Environmental Management. Taking two years off to study in Asia before college opened my eyes to global environmental issues. Now that meetings are live again, plus my part-time job at the Sierra Club, it'll be a juggling act." She paused, then added, "And thank you—and Charlie—for upping my stipend." She met Alexi's eyes, an unspoken understanding passing between them about the fine line they were treading between passion and professionalism.

Alexi smiled, "Want to finish the movie we started last week?"

Chapter 46

Kinda Real

Only a handful of participants showed up this Friday due to another round of COVID concerns. Nevertheless, Fred, ever the catalyst for a lively discussion, opened the meeting with a unique twist.

"I watched *The Truman Show* last night, and it made me think about what we talk about here. Have you seen it?"

"A long time ago," Alexi replied." Want to give us a quick recap so we can discuss it?"

"Sure," he started. "Jim Carrey plays Truman, the unwitting star of a massive reality show. From birth, every moment of his life has been secretly recorded and broadcast without his consent. Everyone around him—his friends, his family, even strangers on the street—are actors on a film set. The movie follows his journey to uncover the truth and plot his escape from a staged life."

"What was your takeaway?" Alexi asked.

"It reminded me of how you say this world is an illusion—that life's a stage, and we're the stars. After watching it, I half-expected to spot hidden cameras documenting me."

Laughter echoed in the nearly empty room.

"The irony of calling it a 'reality' show, right?" Alexi said.

"Truman's experience is a lot like ours. We're born into this world—a true masterpiece of deception—and told it's real despite hints that suggest otherwise. Anything else stand out for you?"

Fred nodded. "His escape. The moment he realizes his life has been scripted, all he wants is something real."

"I loved that part too," Alexi agreed. "He steps off the set, into the streets of LA—into a world full of people who believe their lives are 'authentic.'"

"I know what you mean," Fred added. "Makes you wonder—did he break free or step into a similar charade?"

"Exactly," Alexi said as her creative juices kicked in. "Imagine a sequel, *Truman II*, where he believes his new life in LA is the real McCoy until he realizes he's merely swapped one illusion for another. Then, what? Search for authenticity in new-age bookstores. Or, like me, travel the world, chasing answers, only to find ourselves caught in another stage play—this one wrapped in spiritual jargon."

"Kind of like *Groundhog Day*," Fred mused. "Same endless loop, always searching for the 'real' him, right?"

Alexi nodded. "Well said. The TV audience may want to believe Truman's escape means freedom. But deep down, they know his new freedom is as tenuous as theirs. The streets of LA are as illusory as the set he left behind."

Fred paused, considering. "After the movie, I wondered if there was any hope for me. Am I stuck in an endless loop like Truman?"

Alexi nodded. "It's quite a journey, isn't it? The movie of our lives continues until awakening occurs. Then the star, the temporary limited 'you,' fades into the sunset. What remains is what you have always been—the unmoving screen on which your story unfolds."

Fred frowned. "I never fully got this analogy. So there's no *me* anymore? I disappear? I'm the screen?"

"In a way, yes. It's more that the clinging 'you' fades away. The essence of who you are is the movie screen—always there, ever the same, a silent witness to the story of your life."

She paused, letting the words settle. "Truman still stars in his new LA movie, but now sees his true identity as the screen, untouched by whatever story plays out. He'll still walk the streets of LA, but with a lightness in his stride, realizing his role is nothing but a spectacle to enjoy."

Alexi sensed the difficulty of conveying such profound truths through simple analogies, yet she enjoyed the challenge.

"A Chinese poet described it like this," she added. "At first, I saw mountains as mountains. Then, as I dove deeper into Buddhist teachings, I realized mountains are not mountains. After truly grasping the essence of reality, I again see mountains as mountains."

Leslie joined in, "I've been to countless mind-body-spirit seminars and mulled over its meaning, but honestly, I've never understood it."

Alexi took a deep breath before drawing a parallel between the Chinese poet's journey and Truman's.

"In Truman's early years, he sees everything as real, as his conditioning dictates. This is the stage of unquestioned acceptance, where mountains are simply mountains. Then, a life-altering event shatters this illusion when he discovers his idyllic beach town is nothing more than a TV set. He realizes everything he experiences, including mountains, is not as it appears."

Leslie looked at Alexi, sensing a punchline.

"In the possible sequel, *Truman II*, it's full circle. Truman awakens to the realization that his childhood on a movie set and his new life in LA are just different versions of his story. His pains and sorrows persist, but now he accepts them with a quiet smile. Once again, mountains are simply mountains—but with the understanding that they're both real and illusory, and in this, he finds freedom within life's many paradoxes."

After a silence, Alexi added, "That's my take on it. Others might see it differently."

"So... once Truman sees that life's an illusion, he's finally able to live it—for real?" Leslie asked.

Alexi nodded.

"Wow," Leslie smiled faintly. "That's a little mind-boggling, but I like it. Kinda like what Buddha said—'It's real and unreal and neither one nor the other.'"

"Well said," Alexi replied with a smile. "And you can lose the 'kinda.'" She stood, signaling the meeting's end.

* * *

A cool evening breeze drifted through Alexi's apartment, hinting at the approach of winter. It's Friday, and time for their usual post-meeting meeting. Alexi brought two cups of tea to the living room as Ellie set up her laptop, ready to review her business notes.

"That was fun tonight. Now I want to watch *The Truman Show*," Ellie said, glancing up.

Alexi smiled, handing Ellie a steaming cup. "It was fun, and a lively discussion afterward."

They settled on the couch with Ellie's computer armed and ready to go. "Before we start," Alexi turned to her, "how are you and Michael doing? I haven't seen him at our meetings lately."

"Michael?" she echoed as if suddenly remembering they were dating.

"Yeah, Michael."

Ellie murmured. "We're… fine."

Alexi raised an eyebrow. "You sound like Arlo. What does 'fine' mean?"

Ellie exhaled slowly. "It means 'not so good.'"

"Oh, I see. Would you like to talk about it?"

"To you? Now?"

"Sure, I do it all the time in Friday meetings. I'd say I'm pretty good at it," Alexi smiled, her tone softening. "What's happening?"

"Oh, nothing, just a small thing between us." Ellie hesitated, weighing how much she felt was appropriate to reveal. "Actually, not so small. We haven't been seeing much of each other. It's like the differences seem…."

"Differences?" Alexi asked softly.

"Yeah." Ellie's shoulders sagged a bit. "He's lost interest in your meetings. When we're together, we talk shop, you know, his martial arts, life."

"How does that sit with you?"

"Not great," Ellie admitted, struggling to put her emotions into words. "I'm so involved with you and the meetings, but he zones out when I bring it up." She sighed, staring into her tea. "I thought he was my forever guy. We've been so good together, but..."

"How do you feel about that?" Alexi gently nudged.

"Terribly sad and alone," Ellie whispered, her voice trembling as tears blurred her vision. Suddenly, her restraint cracked, and her words rushed forward like a burst dam. "I mean, we haven't slept together for months. What's that about? When he comes over, he finds an excuse to leave early, and truthfully, I'm relieved. We've only been together for two years. I'm just glad we didn't move in together."

Ellie's hand trembled as she reached for a tissue. In a silent gesture of comfort, Alexi rested Ellie's hand gently on her lap. The moment stretched, wrapping them in a fragile silence, until Ellie's last bit of composure slipped away and she broke into sobs. Alexi drew her close without hesitation, letting Ellie bury her face in her neck.

Ellie took in the embrace and impulsively kissed Alexi's cheek. If Ellie had been conscious of her actions, she would've seen a hundred red flags. That small warning signal in her gut rose almost immediately. Shame? Regret? Who could know in that unguarded moment? Ellie's mind raced, her heart pounded, blood coursing into her head as she struggled to process what she'd done. Before she could make sense of it, her thoughts were silenced as Alexi moved her lips to Ellie's.

Chapter 47

Sally Returns

The following Friday arrived with howling wind and sleet battering the darkened windows. Alexi gestured toward the back of the room. "There's been talk about what's happening in Sally's life. She's here tonight to share an update."

Alexi nodded to Ellie, who brought a chair to the front. As it landed with a soft thud, their eyes met briefly—a quiet acknowledgment of their unspoken connection.

Sally stepped forward, settled into the chair, and offered a warm smile. "Hi, everyone. It's good to be back. After that amazing exercise Alexi led us through, I got a call from my dad—my mom was ill. I went to Denver to be with her during her final days. And no, I didn't ascend into heaven as someone cutely speculated on our site."

Sally paused, eyes drifting to the ceiling as she gathered her thoughts. "My dad has been meditating since before I was born. When I told him about my experience, he asked if I'd gotten enlightened." She chuckled. "I laughed, and I've been doing a lot of that lately. I told him I didn't *get* anything. Instead, it was a day of loss. I lost my fear of the future and, more importantly, that restless part of me that was always searching.

"I used to enjoy reading about spirituality and watching YouTube gurus. I envied them, convinced I could never be like them. And in that, I was correct—I could only be myself. Now, when I read those books, I catch myself mentally correcting the author."

She smiled at the group, aware that each person was processing her words in their own way. "There aren't words that truly capture that shift. By all logic, stepping outside the 'cosmic warehouse' Alexi sometimes talks about, and glimpsing Being, should be impossible—yet it happened. That's why I can't accurately describe it. I can only use language from inside the warehouse, and none of it applies."

She exhaled, shaking her head slightly. "When I try to explain it, people often say, 'I know what you mean; it's like...' And that makes me cringe because what they say back isn't what I meant at all. Now I understand the impossible task Alexi has."

Sally glanced at Alexi, "Sorry, sometimes when I get going... And I don't even know if it makes sense."

Alexi smiled. "Yeah, trying to make it sensible. Does anyone have a question for Sally?"

"I'm a rookie here," Marty said with a half-smile, "but from what I gather, this happened pretty suddenly. I thought this kind of thing was a slow burn—years, maybe lifetimes."

"Same here," Sally said, shaking her head in amazement. "It still boggles my mind. I now believe this 'thing' can only happen in an instant. It's like getting the punchline of a joke and suddenly realizing all past searching didn't matter because I was always that. The exercise with Alexi was a shift so slight it could be overlooked, yet the consequences were monumental."

Marty chuckled. "So, it's like tearing the house apart looking for your glasses, only to realize they've been on your head the whole time?"

"Exactly!" Sally laughed. "And you feel a bit silly."

"So, nothing you did in the past helped?" Marty asked incredulously.

Sally looked at Alexi, who nodded a give-it-a-go. "I don't know the answer to that," she admitted. "This limited mind can't figure it out, but I did nothing to deserve this gift, so I believe it's an accident. But I also believe that by exposing myself to books and these meetings, I became accident-prone."

Alexi chuckled, making a mental note to use that line at a future meeting.

Vince, a regular member of *The Meeting* group, spoke up. "I'm wondering—do you feel different from everyone else now? Special?"

"Great question," Sally said. "Years ago, my dad explained how everything in life is connected. He said a butterfly flapping its wings in the Amazon could stir up a storm in Japan. That stuck with me. The more I find my footing in this new reality, the more I realize we're all part of the same whole."

She paused, "Funnily enough, before my shift, I wanted to be like Alexi or some other brand-name guru. Now I see that I'm not—and never was—different from them. Beneath all our apparent differences, there's a quiet sameness. It's like chocolate and vanilla—different flavors, but still ice cream at the core."

Ruth, an old friend of Sally's, chimed in. "Is it easier to let go of negative feelings about yourself and others?"

Sally smiled warmly. "I don't see 'others' the way I used to. Life still dishes out challenges, but instead of resisting or ignoring my emotions, I accept what's happening instead of arguing with 'what is.' I'm far from perfect, but my perspective has shifted. As Alexi once put it, that 'restless chicken running around in my blouse is no longer there—and what a relief that is."

Alexi chuckled at the memory.

Sally looked to the ceiling, a familiar habit. "I recently read Rudyard Kipling's poem, *If*," she mused, "where he talks about

Triumph and Disaster. I memorized the line: 'Treat those two impostors just the same.'"

Andy was next. "Would you say joy is a part of your life?"

She nodded reflectively. "That's a great word, Andy. Lately, the joy hasn't been over-the-top like when it first happened. Now, it feels more like a whole-body joy. It's certainly not the roller coaster happiness I've been used to. Sadness still happens, but it's against a constant backdrop of peace and contentment."

She paused, glancing around. "A friend asked if it's love. I told him no. But after a moment, I said, 'You know, it's like love.' Sometimes, it feels like it wants to ooze through my pores. I thank the universe daily for this gift of a human body."

Andy followed up. "You said you laugh a lot now. Is that tied to joy?"

"Hmm? You're making me think," she said, pausing. "I'd say they're similar. When I look in a certain way at my surroundings, I see things as ephemeral—that's a word I learned recently," she added with a satisfied smile. "It's like nothing feels so heavy or serious anymore. A lightness allows me to appreciate what I see more fully." She paused again, eyes glancing upward. "I notice the hidden beauty of what I perceive, and that brings my inner joy to the surface."

Sally scanned the room, taking in the engaged faces. "This whole adventure is so strange that I started writing about the experience from the fullness of life. I always imagined something grand would happen—bells and whistles stuff. But it was the opposite. During that exercise with Alexi, nothing seemed to happen, yet that 'nothing' ended the search that consumed so much of my energy." She paused. "I always thought people who talked like this were making it up…"

Sally gave Alexi a sheepish glance. "Oh, not you, Alexi."

Alexi laughed, and Sally added, "But in a fashion, it's all made up—just not how I expected it to be."

Sally sat for a moment, then looked at Alexi. "I want to thank you with all my heart. I now feel I've started and ended my journey simultaneously."

"Thank you, Sally," Alexi replied with a warm smile. Sally returned her smile, hand on heart, before returning to her seat.

"I've had numerous requests for you to do this," Alexi beamed, "and I can unequivocally say you're not making this up. I'd say you fabricated your life and words prior to that exercise. However, after a while, there's a normalization. Life isn't lived in the beyond. It's more like the beyond starts finding a home in this human form. And, as you say, what a relief that is."

Chapter 48

4th of July 2022

"Welcome!" Alexi cheerfully opened the meeting. It was the first Friday gathering in more than two years where no one was wearing a mask. "It's great to see so many faces—literally—especially on this long July Fourth weekend."

She paused for a beat. "St. Cloud knows how to throw a great Fourth of July bash, and this year's is bound to top them all. But before we get too caught up in fireworks and funnel cakes, Ray's been asking—more than once—if we can talk about free will. Seems like an appropriate time for it. But first, Ellie's got a few announcements."

Ellie jumped up, a playful energy radiating from her. Decked out in an American flag pirate bandana, she ditched her usual professional persona and channeled her zany side. "Indeed, I do. Tonight's meeting will be a tad shorter 'cause Ralph and Rita are hosting a pre-4th shindig at their lakeside cabin. Bring your dancing shoes! But wait, there's more. Tomorrow, we're taking over our usual softball field 'cause our friends from Des Moines dared to challenge us. I'm counting on you, your clan, and all your heavy-hitter friends to join us. There's a flyer on the back table with the juicy details. Spoiler alert: no teatime tonight."

"That was impressive." Alexi looked at Ellie with admiration. "You certainly sold me."

Good-natured laughter filled the room, many sporting the red, white, and blue headbands Ellie handed out, setting the tone for a memorable evening.

Alexi turned to Ray, wondering if the 40 or so attendees would be up for a discussion, especially about free will, but she decided to press on: "Ray, you're batting first."

"Thanks, Alexi, it's a simple question—do we have free will?"

Ray's so-called 'simple' question and the room's lively energy sparked another wave of laughter. When it quietened, Alexi got down to business. "Ah, the classic question that inevitably pops up in gatherings like this: do we have free will, or is everything determined? I asked Lyam about this, and he said no one can have free will until they're enlightened—then they don't need it anymore."

Ray smiled, "I like that. Wish I could meet him someday."

"He also warned me never to discuss free will because it's a wormhole that'll get you lost in space," she added.

"I get it," Ray persisted. "After my online searches, I realize it's like nailing Jell-O to a wall. But I've been obsessed with this for years. I'd love to hear your take."

"Okay, let me give it a shot—without setting off too many fireworks. First, we have to ask the right question: Is there free will, or do I have free will? My answer to the first? Yes, there is free will. Not just for humans, but for plants and animals too. Every organism chooses to express itself to its fullest.

However, 'Do I have free will?' is another story. That assumes that there's an entity, a 'me,' that can choose. It's this skinny word 'I,'—the subject of nearly every thought—that's the trickster."

She noticed a few distracted faces but continued. "'I' and free will are not compatible. Phrases like 'I am sad,' 'I am thinking,' 'I love running' are ways to identify who we are or what we do.

But before we qualify our true self with anything from the world, 'I am' is free, unbound. When the 'I' identifies with thoughts or objects, the 'I' we believe ourselves to be becomes trapped, defined by what it perceives. And that 'I' is no longer free."

Alexi looked at Ray, hoping this would end the conversation. "Does this do it for you?"

Ray nodded but pressed on. "Are you saying there's more than one me?"

"That's the dilemma we face when diving into existential waters," Alexi said. "It seems like there are two I's or self's—the unchanging, unbounded self and the one that shifts with the tides of circumstances or objects of perception. There's only one 'I,' one I am, one true self.

"For the purpose of discussing free will, it helps to distinguish between two aspects of self: the 'silent self,' which is ever-present and free of history or future projections, and the 'personal self,' the ever-changing, controlling self we recognize in our daily lives. From the perspective of the silent self, things happen freely without conscious cause. Each thought or action is original, spontaneous, and fresh."

Alexi glanced at Ray, who was jotting notes, and continued, "Contrast that with thoughts or actions arising from the personal self, the limited 'I.' These aren't spontaneous or creative. They're influenced by past experiences and tangled in a loop of judgment and commentary. This 'I' gives the illusion of being the doer, of having free will, but it's just reacting to circumstances."

She paused. "Animals aren't concerned about whether their actions are determined, moral, or free. When birds migrate, we call it instinct, but when humans fly south for the winter, we call it free will. The ego makes this distinction to feel important and in control. The personal self, or ego, only *seems* to choose freely, but is always a step behind. It can't experience the world directly. It only comments on what already happened."

Alexi noticed some participants were ready to party, but Ray remained focused.

"Thank you, Alexi. That was more impressive than anything I've read. But one last question: from what you've said, it seems you're on Team Free Will, even if it clashes with the idea of a personal self."

Alexi smiled, knowing her response would never fly at a Free-Will Seminar.

"I'd say I'm a fan of freedom, not free will. But look—what's the point of not believing? I 'choose' to believe in free will, fully aware it's mental gymnastics. Whatever we choose, it's all the same, a reflection of Absolute Being. So, choose away."

Ray hesitated, then leaned forward.

"I feel you're sick of this subject, but one last question—honestly. What about psychics who can see the future? That makes me think all is determined."

"I believe some seers can glimpse the future, but only sometimes. They see probable futures, but these shift with each next choice. Each decision, drawn from the warehouse of life's infinite possibilities, marks a new beginning."

Alexi paused and looked at Ray. "Is there a ray of hope here?"

Ray smiled, and Alexi continued, "My intention is not to sway you into believing in free will or determinism but to show how useless and unproductive the pursuit of this topic can be. Beyond these concepts lies the reality that we are both free and determined, and these two realities paradoxically coexist. Enough. I can see everyone is ready to party."

Chapter 49

Cosmic Warehouse

The gentle ring of the meditation bell faded into the room, lit only by the soft glow of twilight filtering through the curtains. Tonight, it's Morris who broke the shared silence and started the conversation.

"I found last week's meeting on free will interesting," he began. "Toward the end, you mentioned something about a warehouse of life. Can you elaborate on that?"

"I did skip over that hurdle quickly," Alexi acknowledged. "I believe I was talking about how limited our attention is because we only see a small slice of this immense creation that's always present."

Making abstract ideas tangible had always been challenging for Alexi, who was constantly searching for ways to translate life's most fundamental truths into practical understanding. She drew in a slow breath and began.

"Imagine the universe as a vast warehouse containing every possible object and experience. Anything you can name exists in the warehouse: every thought, object, and moment. Better yet, everyone, close your eyes for a moment and picture yourselves stepping into a cosmic warehouse, carrying only a small flashlight. Its narrow beam lights up only a tiny slice of what's there. Whatever the light illuminates becomes your present reality—maybe your car, a favorite vacation memory, or even you sitting here in this room. Are you with me?"

She glanced around the room, catching nods encouraging her to continue. Alexi discovered that group exercises were an excellent way to talk about, as Lyam would say, 'the essential facts of life.'

"Imagine attending a seminar in this warehouse and being handed a more powerful light. Suddenly, you can perceive life's subtleties and understand more of the interconnectedness within the warehouse. You start noticing patterns and grasping the bigger picture. You wonder why others don't see it the way you do—but of course, they're still using their small flashlights.

"Finally, a great teacher hands you an enormous light, bright enough to illuminate the entire warehouse. Congratulations—after lifetimes of searching, you've made it—you're enlightened. You can now speak fluently about multiple dimensions and tap into knowledge far beyond the reach of your friends. You've arrived! And yet... something feels off.

"After a thousand years of mystical powers and long talks with God, everything starts to feel a little… meh. Sensing your existential funk, your spouse suggests, 'How about I make you an apple pie from that tree over there? You know—the one with the charming snake lounging in the branches."

Laughter rippled through the group. Alexi remembered a piece of advice from a motivational speaker: *Get them to laugh, and they'll continue to listen.*

"We can get lost in the warehouse, searching endless aisles for money, power, relationships, knowledge, or self-improvement—hoping something will satisfy us. But we overlook the obvious, the light that brings everything to life. It's the light that appreciates its contents and illuminates our bodies, thoughts, and feelings. The light is the silent self, the essence of who we are."

Alexi paused, letting her words settle.

"As the light of awareness becomes brighter, objects fade into the background. The light floods the warehouse of your mind, and everything is seen as an expression of divine radiance, divine love. You realize there is only light, and you are that light—the source of everything. Who you are is beautiful, endless light, the light of God, Being, Wholeness, Consciousness, the totality of everything that exists—love, joy, and peace."

"Hmm," Morris reflected a moment before speaking. "So, you're saying God or Being is also in the warehouse."

"Excellent!" Alexi replied. "You've found that which is not a property of the warehouse."

"But you said anything that can be named is included in the warehouse. I just named Being."

"True, but we previously discussed Being, God, or Absolute Reality as that which is nameless, beyond this relative universe. We only use these terms so we can discuss them in our conversations. What you know about God isn't God. Everything you know about God and Being, even your deepest spiritual insights, are in the warehouse, but the essence of God and Being exists beyond it."

"But not actual God or Being?"

Alexi laughed. "Morris, I'm impressed by your pithy questions. All that exists is Being, so in that sense, Being is in the warehouse. It's like the ocean. Waves rise and fall and are an aspect of the ocean, but not the whole ocean. Maybe it's better to say the warehouse hovers in Being or exists within Being, making its contents possible. The warehouse and its contents are a reflection of Being and only appear real."

Morris, now retired from teaching Chinese Buddhism at the U of M, recently found his way to Alexi's meetings. Alexi was thrilled because he brought a rare depth to the conversation, something uncommon most evenings.

"What about the light?" he asked. "Is that in the warehouse? Isn't the light also a thing?"

"The light consisting of waves and photons isn't what I'm referring to—this is a shadowless light. I say 'light' because it lights our world, enabling us to perceive. Perhaps it's better to say silent awareness or the invisible light of Being. Once it's understood that you are this light, you're not just a wave in the ocean; you are the ocean."

Morris nodded a silent thank you.

Alexi glanced across the room and noticed some blank stares. She was about to wrap things up when Fred spoke.

"This explains why Einstein struggled with a unified field theory, right? He was stuck in the warehouse, thinking that's all there was. Perhaps he wasn't familiar with the light of Being."

Alexi nodded. "I agree. He often spoke of God as a concept, but all concepts are contained in the warehouse. He could theorize about the nature of creation, but possibly never had a direct experience of awakening to the light behind it all."

She paused before continuing, happy Fred brought up this topic. "That's a scientist's challenge. No matter how brilliant, they're bound by the language of the relative world—numbers, equations, thoughts, words. The only language that serves here is silence, where true understanding lies beyond concepts and theories, beyond the limits of the warehouse."

"Sort of the language of the Void?" Fred mused aloud.

"Exactly."

"So then, a unified theory is impossible?" Fred's thoughts raced, not wanting to let the thread go. "And all Einstein's effort was of no avail.

"No, it's possible," Alexi replied without hesitation. "It's so simple that the mind overlooks it, especially brilliant minds. It can only be grasped by what lies beyond the mind."

Fred paused, half wondering if she was joking. A skeptical laugh slipped out. "Okay! You have a theory?"

"If I were to write an equation for the unified theory of the universe, I'd say: nothing is the same as everything—zero equals infinity."

Fred laughed, but let the simplicity sink in. After a moment, his face lit up. "That's good. I like it. But what would you say when a scientist asks for proof?"

"Once I got their attention, I'd take it a step further and rewrite it as: '0 = infinity = wholeness = love.' Nothing and everything are the same; all is one, and its nature is love. Then, I'd tell them to leave their mind on the lab table and sit quietly. The proof can only happen in silence. Sometimes, the simplest things are the hardest to grasp."

Fred grinned. "The more I think about it, the more I like your equation. Scientists say everything arises from a void, the quantum vacuum state, then instantly decays and disappears."

"In Indian cosmology," Alexi replied, slipping comfortably into familiar territory from her time in India, "it's believed that everything is created and destroyed in that same fashion. We don't have words for finer levels of creation, nor do they. They believed this area of life was so close to God that they envisioned a divine trinity, instead of equations. They equate Brahman with Being or Absolute Reality. From Brahman comes Brahma, the creator; Vishnu, the maintainer; and Shiva, the destroyer."

"I read about that before, but it never clicked like now," Fred added excitedly. "Now I get it when you talk about emptiness and say everything is nothing. Everything, including us, is a quantum fluctuation arising from an empty vacuum state."

"Yes, this meeting, this life, this universe is a quantum dream."

"So, when you say all this is an illusion, you're talking science."

Alexi nodded. "Indian mythology also states that the universe's life cycle is finite, as is Brahma, its creator. This aligns with the scientific theory that the universe and its contents expand, until eventually, all that will be left is space. And space without objects is no space at all—just emptiness."

Fred leaned back, shaking his head slowly. "I find this conversation fascinating."

"It's like a Rubik's cube," Alexi said. "Once you figure out how it works, it's no longer interesting. The puzzle of the universe will keep scientists entertained until they realize the answer won't be found inside the warehouse. When the light of awareness silences their thinking mind, even for a timeless moment, it reveals a truth beyond the confines of science. And what is that truth? An inexpressible fullness, where every answer quietly resides."

The meeting lasted longer than usual, but many of the vacuous faces now came alive. Just as Ellie stood to make her announcements, Phil asked. "What about other universes, the multi-universe?"

"Yeah," Alexi smiled, "This was a fun discussion, but I think one universe is enough for tonight."

Chapter 50

Another Funeral

It was a crisp fall day, three and a half years after Alice died, and once more, Alexi, Mira, and Lyam found themselves in the somber atmosphere of a funeral. This time, they were at the crematorium for Alexi's father, Ben. After a brief unceremonial ceremony and the usual exchange of condolences, Ben's brother headed off to catch a flight back to a life interrupted by death.

"It's a beautiful day," Lyam observed, his voice cutting through the quietude. "Shall we go for a walk? There's a park across the street."

"I'd love that," Alexi responded, turning to Mira. "Mom?" Mira nodded in quiet agreement.

They strolled in silence for a few minutes, until Alexi spoke. "Death is a strange phenomenon. During one of my trips to India, I visited Varanasi. Everything there is so in-your-face. One evening, I sat for hours by the Ganges, watching mourners carry their loved ones on biers to the cremation grounds. Seeing the bodies burn was transforming. When it was over, their ashes were swept into the river. Compared to that, Dad's farewell felt almost subdued."

After heading down a slope to the river, Lyam turned to

Mira. "How are you doing with all this?"

"Of course, I'm sad but also confused. This past week, sitting with Ben, I kept sifting through memories, wondering how we fared. He could often be in his own world, but he was faithful, and there wasn't all the drama that some of my friends go through in their marriages."

Never one for superficiality, Alexi asked softly, "This might not be a good time, but I've often wondered why you picked him?"

Mira answered without hesitation, "Security. There were so many things I admired about your father. His steady presence was a contrast to the mercurial men I had dated. I didn't have much guidance in love and relationships when I was younger." She shrugged. "Possibly, I overcompensated in the safety category."

Lyam paused, his expression softening. "I'm sorry I wasn't there for you."

"Thanks," Mira whispered.

After a few more paces, Mira turned to Alexi. "My biggest regret is that you and Ben never bonded as I'd hoped— possibly because he was sixteen years older than me. He was great with his students, but that skill didn't translate to family. Our conversations always felt somewhat unfulfilling. But you, you filled that gap in your late teens. You were precocious that way."

Alexi grinned. "Precocious or a thorn in your side?" Her smile faded as her thoughts drifted to her father. "I'm trying to process this myself. Dad was a fine person. I felt no antagonism toward him, as I did with Alice. But you're right—we never connected. If I had a do-over, I'd try harder with both."

After a brief silence, Alexi asked, "Did you love Dad?"

Mira gazed over the river. "I've asked myself that many times, but truth be told, I don't know. I always knew I wanted a child, and stability was my mantra. Not very romantic, huh? I believe Alice's impact on my life runs deeper than I care to admit."

"Oh my god," Alexi blurted, "did you hear that? A loon call the moment you mentioned Alice. I've got goosebumps."

"Me too. There aren't many loons around here anymore."

They watched the loon dive for fish, its unpredictable surfacing mirroring the currents of their feelings. Sunlight slipped through the clouds, painting the landscape in autumn hues. A barge drifted down the river, probably carrying corn or wheat bound for the Gulf.

Mira shifted her gaze to Lyam, "Okay, since it's true confessions, what about you? Were you ever in love? Did you love Alice?"

Lyam, caught off-guard by the sudden shift of attention, hesitated, "I thought I loved Alice, but at nineteen, I was confusing love with passion."

Mira's voice carried a hint of playfulness. "Arlo was also nineteen in your book. How could you write so beautifully about his love for Zoe?"

"Because I wrote that after discovering love in my late forties."

Mira and Alexi exchanged a curious look. The idea of Alexi's grandfather, the embodiment of wisdom, having a romance felt almost impossible to imagine. Like children stumbling upon a treasure chest of hidden stories, their eyes silently urged him to reveal more.

"Alright, I get it," Lyam conceded with a resigned chuckle. "I moved to Crestone not long after Alexi was born. That town was an eye-opener—just saying."

All three laughed as Lyam threw in Zoe's catchphrase from his book.

"Crestone's new-age vibes and eclectic spiritual scene felt odd at first. About a year in, I was hiking up the Mountain to Willow Lake—a beautiful five-hour round trip. Midway, I stopped for a snack and saw this incredible being coming down the trail.

She stopped and introduced herself as Kay. She mentioned she noticed me in the coffee shop the day before. We chatted for a few minutes, and I didn't want it to end, but I was determined to make it to the lake for a swim before it got too late. I stood, ready to leave, hoping I would see her again. But before I started up-hill, she asked if she could join me. She said her swim earlier was so refreshing, she would like an encore."

Mira laughed, yet wished she could have been so bold in her dating days. "You never noticed her, yet she appeared as this incredible presence?"

"It's like that with some people. They radiate a certain energy or frequency that stirs subtle feelings beneath the surface. I call it a proper mix of heaven and earth. When this happens, I expand my perception and look closer for some connection."

Lyam's eyes lowered, his words fading into a hush. Sensing the weight of his pause, Mira gently nudged him, aware of the delicate nature of her prodding. "And?"

Lyam exhaled and began. "Kay lived in Santa Fe, but once her youngest flew the nest, she'd come to Crestone each year for six weeks of biking, climbing, and spiritual retreats. A few months after our hike to Willow Lake, she moved here. We lived together for the next four and a half years. I always believed God's presence shone the brightest in silent meditation, but Kay taught me otherwise. She showed me that God lives through her, through me, through everything. She designed the popular poster that reads, *We are all a walking God.* Kay was a tantric yoga master who revealed the many faces of the divine in every facet of life. You asked how I wrote about Arlo's first kiss. Now you know."

A trace of heartache crossed Lyam's face. Mira lowered her voice. "You keep speaking in the past tense, and that scares me."

"Kay was an exceptional biker and hiker. Each year, she would climb the three tallest peaks around Crestone. We just returned from a bike tour in Oregon, and she had yet to climb Kit Carson Peak. Usually, we'd climb together, but I had to work. She had a one-day window before the first storm in October. I dropped her off at the trailhead at three in the morning, plenty of time for a round trip."

Lyam's gaze dropped. "But the Mountain had its own plans. The storm came in earlier and heavier than expected. Kit Carson has one notoriously tricky section during the descent. She apparently missed the correct route in the snow."

Mira and Alexi pulled Lyam into a tight embrace. A quiet settled over their surroundings, as if the world had paused to pay its respects.

"I loved every aspect of her," Lyam said softly. "Kay sowed the seeds that illuminated my life, opening me to the beauty of human connection. A year after her death, Charlie made it possible for me to bring those lessons to life."

Lyam looked at Alexi and Mira, his heart quietly thanking Kay for giving him the tools to be a meaningful presence in the lives of these two remarkable women.

"Whew!" Alexi exhaled, wondering why she'd never asked about his past during their many balloon and bike rides. "And Kay—Arlo and Zoe's teacher in the book is her. Right?"

"Yes, she lives on in the book—and in you. Those drawings of Arlo and Zoe in the book were her creations. Kay was a gifted illustrator and dreamed of creating an animated film. On our hikes, we'd conjure up stories of adventure around them. I simply fulfilled her vision in book form."

They stood in silence, gazing across the Mississippi. Mira and Alexi wondered how much more they would discover about Lyam in the coming years. Then, without further prompting, Lyam continued, "My longing for Kay's bodily form persists, but understanding that her essence—along with Ben's, and Alice's—is universal love, softens the ache. Kay taught me to cherish life as a gift I'm grateful to immerse myself in."

Three generations, linked by blood and memories, stood at the overlook, watching the loon glide across the water. An unspoken connection deepened between them as strangers passed by, absorbed in their own world.

They slowly wandered down an unmarked path, each lost in silent reflections. Then, with a mischievous glint, Lyam poked Alexi in the ribs. "And what about you, Alexi? What's happening in your love life?"

Alexi laughed. "Touché! Now we're getting personal—but I like personal. As you both know, Ellie and I have been a couple for nearly two years, and we now wonder if we fell into each other's laps because of COVID. We love each other, and all is good, but we're starting to ask ourselves if good is good enough?"

"Can I weigh in on this?" Mira asked. "I always wanted to be a model for love, but I missed out on that with Alice. Sometimes, I felt like I was wearing an 'inadequate' sign around my neck."

"But Mom," Alexi cut in, "you're anything but inadequate. And I do have a loving relationship with Ellie. I don't believe I'm gay—maybe bi."

Alexi glanced at Lyam. "As Mom knows, I had a somewhat serious relationship with Roger in High School. And if you are wondering, Roger was the first guy I had sex with—sex but not love, as I imagined. Each time I read that chapter where Arlo declares his love for Zoe, tears streamed down my face.. Maybe you ruined me."

Lyam smiled as Alexi continued, "The only one I had a real crush on in college was my physics professor. Mom thought I was looking for a father figure." She turned to Lyam, warmth in her gaze. "But aside from him, I'd take our conversations over any guy I ever dated."

As they circled back to their cars, the sun dipped behind a cloud, and it started to drizzle. They hugged—a silent acknowledgment of all they shared. Mira offered a final reflection. "Who knows what death draws out in people?"

Chapter 51

Nothing to Get

After twenty minutes of meditation, the room settled into a calm stillness. At the end of an unusually long silence, Phil finally spoke up. "I want to thank you eternally for these meetings. I find them very insightful."

Alexi chuckled playfully. "Eternally? Do you know what eternity is?"

"A long, long time. Endless." Phil, ever the analytical mind, answered.

"That's the usual take," Alexi bantered. "Eternal has nothing to do with time. Eternal has no boundaries and is timeless—no past, no future. There is only the eternal now, always the same and always different. So, when you thank me, I'm grateful —eternally."

"O-k-a-y." Phil sputtered, then shifted gears. "I've heard you say that this world's an illusion and nothing matters, correct?"

Alexi arched an eyebrow, "I believe I said that nothing *ultimately* matters, but I feel you're heading somewhere with this.

Phil glanced around the room with a grin. "By the way, Alexi knows me well. We were co-teachers at the same school—Alexi Biology, me Physics."

Alexi smiled, "Yes, we've had many spirited exchanges over the years."

Phil continued, "So if everything is an illusion and meaningless, why can't I lead these sessions? After all, I've studied Eastern philosophy for over 35 years."

"Aha, before my grand entrance!" Alexi quipped. "Your request is sound, and if it's about dialectics, you win. You may have gotten an 'A' in logic, but in these meetings, the mind becomes humbled and can become your nemesis. If you were up here, people would leave because you'd try to make sense of it all. In a way, it's logical—until it isn't."

"But I *do* understand what you're saying," Phil insisted.

"You do?" Alexi challenged. "Understanding can be a crutch that keeps the mind engaged and prevents it from Understanding, with a capital U. When awakening happens, logic becomes irrelevant."

Phil frowned. "But you understand it."

Alexi shook her head. "No, I don't. Not in the way you think. And neither did Buddha. The words I use are pointers, meant to stir your imagination and direct your attention beyond the limits of language."

"Then why talk if it makes no sense?"

"Now, that's a great question." Alexi nodded, "Why talk? I asked Lyam that same question, expecting him to say it's only for our entertainment. Instead, he said that sometimes words are necessary to satisfy the mind and correct misunderstandings."

Phil frowned, struggling to connect the dots. "That sounds contradictory to what I've heard you say before that words are a distraction."

"Eternity encompasses contradictions."

Phil exhaled as he regrouped. "Okay, here's my point. It seems that some here 'get it,' as if there's some kind of exclusive 'got it' club. A quiet laugh rippled through the room, mirroring

Phil's bewilderment.

Alexi often found herself at a familiar crossroads in meetings like this. She learned that inviting reflection on the mind's limits can open the door to deeper insight. In rare moments of stillness—when thoughts stop their endless gymnastics and the need to 'get it' fades—a clear, timeless awareness emerges, pure and free, beyond concepts and imagination.

"And why do you want to get this?" Alexi asked.

"Because I want to be included."

"I see, but this wanting reinforces your stuckness and exclusion."

"Then what to do?"

"Nothing. It's already done."

"That sounds like a catch-22."

"In a way, it is," Alexi smiled. "It's like that cartoon where God says, 'If I made it easy, it wouldn't be any fun.' What is it you want?"

"I don't know, but after talking to Sally, it seems I'm missing something."

"Didn't you hear Sally say there's nothing to get?" Alexi's tone was light but firm. "Nothing is missing. The real issue is you're getting too much. The only thought keeping you stuck is, 'There has to be something more out there, and I want it.' Chasing the next big thing feeds the ego and keeps you stuck in an endless cycle."

A trace of frustration crept into Phil's voice. "I've heard that before, but there's a whole industry based on enlightenment."

"That's a novel perspective," Alexi grinned. "An industry. I like it. Enlightenment means removing the veil that clouds the ever-present light. Your insistence on getting something makes the veil more opaque."

Phil took a deep breath and shifted course, realizing Alexi was not going to toss him a carrot. "I read once, 'I am the light that illumines all.'"

Alexi nodded. "Beautiful. There's no darkness, only degrees of light. The veil is like clouds blocking the sun—the more transparent the clouds, the clearer the vision. But all this is merely a way of talking about it. This process is unpredictable, and each realization is unique. The veil may lift gradually, but at some point, it will be obliterated like a supernova, erasing all traces of your previous illusory self. There's no formula, so that opens the door for endless discussion. Phil, are you good? Are you ready to lead next week's meeting?"

Phil cracked a smile. "I'm fine—but maybe not next week." His tone softened. "Really, though… it's been something watching how far you've come since we taught together."

Alexi smiled warmly. "People often have misconceptions about enlightenment, thinking it's some elevated state where you become a 'super citizen' with gobs of wisdom. There's no becoming a perfect Buddhist or perfect whatever. Everything is as it is. In the grand movie of our lives, no role is minor or imperfect."

She paused before continuing, "Enlightenment doesn't make you flawless—it allows you to embrace your flaws. It's not extraordinary; it only seems that way until you realize it isn't. Enlightenment isn't about acquiring profound experiences or finding some ideal Shangri-La. The invitation is to recognize what's happening right now. Don't overlook the present moment."

* * *

Alexi and Ellie settled onto the couch for their usual Friday night meeting. Between them, steaming mugs of tea contrasted with the cool glow of an Excel spreadsheet on Ellie's laptop. Alexi's apartment was a cheerful mess of wrapping paper and unboxed gifts strewn around a modest artificial tree. As Alexi turned off the Enya album, Ellie glanced up. "Business as usual, or should we talk about that belligerent Fundamentalist Christian?"

Alexi shrugged. "Can you go over the details again? Sounds a lot like that incident a year ago."

"This might be different. The guy's name is Abel. Remember him? Fred and Bob had to escort him out of the room this summer. Yesterday, he posted in our comments section and accused you of some pretty dark stuff. I deleted it, but he said he'll *SPILL THE BEANS*—all caps—unless you contact him soon."

Alexi frowned. "Spill the beans on what? You think… us?"

Ellie raised an eyebrow.

"You're right, this doesn't sound good. But what could he say other than that we're lovers?"

Ellie looked up from her computer. "I don't know, but it smells ominous. Anyway, I'm not sure what to do or what we can do." She paused before adding, "Oh, I forgot to mention, my brother's coming home. It'll be our first family Christmas in four years."

"That's great. I enjoyed meeting him this summer," Alexi replied. "I wish you could be at the retreat, but thanks for bringing Fred up to speed. I don't know what we would do without him," she exhaled. "I'm a bit distracted. Maybe we should chill if there's nothing else urgent."

Ellie's smile was thoughtful as she closed her laptop before snuggling up on the couch next to Alexi.

Chapter 52

Christmas Retreat

Nestled in the heart of Minnesota, a secluded resort sits among tall pines beside a frozen lake. Time slows here, offering a welcome break from the hustle of daily life, providing space for reflection and a deeper connection with the self.

Organizing the retreat was no small feat, especially without Ellie. But Fred and his team rose to the occasion, handling last-minute hiccups, including a few frozen pipes. As the fourteen participants settled in, Alexi took a moment to thank everyone who helped make this first-ever, week-long silent retreat possible. Aware that most arrived after a long drive, she kept the first evening brief.

"I see everyone's brought a blanket," Alexi began, her voice calm against the blustery weather outside. "Fear not—by tomorrow, it should be toasty in here. For now, a warm welcome to each of you."

She scanned the eclectic mix of participants, inviting them to reflect on the true meaning of retirement—no matter their age. With a calm presence, she drew parallels between the mental adjustments of retirement and the journey into silence they were about to undertake. The retreat's schedule mixed meetings, yoga, meditation, and nature walks, all designed to support this inner journey.

With the resort's natural beauty as a backdrop, Alexi's vision of creating a space for stillness and reflection had come to life. "This week," she said, "no matter your situation, let's step away from the world's noise and let life's quieter rhythms unfold. It's a time to differentiate between idle daydreaming and conscious restful alertness that fosters silence. Let's make this week an early retirement for everyone—and allow life to breathe."

* * *

By the last day of the retreat, the resort resonated with a palpable silence. Alexi was puzzled when a text from Ellie popped up that evening. At 9 PM, after the final session wrapped up, she called her back—and Ellie immediately dove in.

"I don't like disrupting your retreat, but something devastating is in the works, and it would be good to think about it on your drive back."

"Are you okay?" Alexi asked with concern.

"No, we are not. It's about that Christian guy."

Alexi's stomach tightened, a prelude to what she was expecting to hear. Ellie took a breath and continued, "It's about Abel—the fundamentalist Fred and Rob threw out of the meeting. Remember when we accidentally sent our email list to the entire contact group? His name was on that list."

"I do. Is there a problem with that? "Alexi asked, a sense of foreboding creeping in.

"Apparently, Abel was able to…" Ellie trailed off as Alexi chuckled at the unintended wordplay. Ellie's annoyance was felt over the air waves, sensing that Alexi was not grasping the seriousness of this situation.

"Alexi," Ellie became more forceful, "he bugged our hotel

room in Des Moines during your book signing and meeting with Jill's group. I suspect it was in the flowers sent to our room. On Christmas Day, we both got an unwelcome gift from him—a transcript of our entire conversation. I know you didn't take your computer, so the message is there waiting. Embarrassing doesn't begin to describe what he recorded.

"Ouch," Alexi winced.

Ellie pressed on, sure she now had Alexi's full attention. "His terms are for you to end all meetings and admit you are a blasphemer, or he'll post our conversation to our email list and write an article for *The St. Cloud Times*."

A lump formed in Alexi's throat as the weight of the situation sank in. "Isn't that illegal? And who would even care about our private conversation?"

"It's undoubtedly illegal, and I don't believe *The Times* would print it, but what can be done?" Ellie's voice sharpened. "This isn't Sweden, so I imagine some would be more than upset—they'd be downright mortified. Can you imagine how we would be perceived at meetings? We said some very embarrassing stuff in that hotel—the thought gives me chills. I replay some of our bedroom conversations and wonder if your meetings will be filtered through a lens of sex. I believe you'd lose a bunch of them—probably even me."

It's clear that Ellie thought through the ramifications, and none of them led to a happy ending.

Ellie murmured, "How could he be so cruel?"

Alexi saw the writing on the wall and became more contained. "Look, during the Inquisition, sadists hid behind religion. Comparatively, our situation is a walk in the park. And we did talk about our relationship having a finish line, didn't we?"

"We did. But not like this," Ellie paused, her voice softening. "I believe this is our wake-up call. I'm flying back the day after tomorrow. Let's talk then."

"Okay," Alexi conceded. "I need to sleep on this—if I can. I want to call Lyam before it gets too late."

For Alexi, falling asleep usually came as easily as flipping a switch. But not tonight. Her thoughts drifted to Lyam. *I'm lucky to feel comfortable confiding in him. What an incredible well of wisdom and understanding.* When she shared her story with him, she could tell he was kind enough to hide a laugh, saying only, "Oh, I totally empathize with your situation."

Lyam's time at the rez had its own twists. His life was upended by an unstable woman who had been impossible to deal with. *He hadn't lied to Mom and me about his relationship with Alice,* she thought, *but like Ellie and me, he sidestepped the truth. Transparency has been a core value for me, but now Ellie and I wrestle with it—like politicians who promise openness yet only reveal what serves their interests.*

But life isn't a neatly written script by Mister Rogers. The plot often has rough edges, forcing compromising choices, each as thorny and unforgiving as the next. I love obstacle bike races, but dealing with fanatical people raises the bar on the word "challenge." Lyam's words were fresh in her mind: "If you're playing softball, expect curveballs, and don't count on the umpire calling them your way." They laughed when Alexi told him that hit home for her.

Even with all the talk at her meetings about life's illusions, Alexi knew those illusions still demanded attention. After all, a movie without drama quickly loses its charm. She smirked at the thought: *A guru caught in a sex scandal? That would make a great film—except it's practically a cliché.*

A final whimsical thought drifted by before she fell asleep: *Ironically, this retreat's theme is retirement. Let me enjoy the last day and let life breathe.*

Chapter 53

A New Beginning

It was Wednesday evening, two days shy of Friday's gathering. Alexi and Ellie were sitting next to each other at the head of the room, their usual lighthearted ease replaced by a heavy silence. Around them, familiar chatter weaved through the air—talk of the Christmas retreat, New Year's adventures, and the latest buzz about Fred and Steve's upcoming birthday bash on February 12th. As they all found seats, Julie joked about Alexi and Ellie's 'new seating arrangement.'

Alexi cleared her throat, and the lively energy shifted as a hint of unease filled the air. "Some may have noticed that Ellie and I are quite somber tonight. We have some troubling news to share that will soon come your way. Ellie and I have been in a relationship for nearly two years, and we will be exposed in the next few weeks. In light of this, we've decided to suspend all future meetings after Friday."

The room fell into stunned silence, as if everyone was holding their breath, waiting for clarity before they could breathe again.

"Ellie, Fred, and I are here tonight to give you the details." Alexi's steady voice carried an undertone of vulnerability.

The air thickened as the group collectively braced for what

was coming next. Fred, Alexi's ride-share partner to and from the retreat, was the only one privy to the events hinted at until now. His relationship with Alexi was one of a long and caring friendship. His calm, practical nature balanced Alexi's more impulsive tendencies.

Fred began unraveling the story, his voice thick with emotion. He reminded everyone about last summer, when Abel was ushered out of the meeting and the *Reply All* email sent by mistake. His words resonated with the bittersweet memories they all shared. As he spoke, there was a sense of finality, like the closing of a cherished chapter. His gaze swept across the room, lingering on familiar faces, silently acknowledging their shared journey.

Julie's shock was evident, her voice softer than usual. She pointed out Alexi's unique status in St. Cloud, a mix of fringe celebrity and spiritual outlier, and the hurdles this might pose in such a conservative city. Beneath her words was a clear sense of loss, a reluctance to let go. Her eyes met Alexi's, holding a blend of admiration and sadness—a quiet tribute to their friendship and the spiritual insights Alexi's meetings brought to her life.

Mary, who was openly gay, was next. "I'm all over the place, emotionally. There's nothing wrong with a loving relationship, love is love. Anyway, some of us already suspected it. But why keep it a secret? Why end the meetings?"

"We didn't intend to keep it a secret," Ellie responded with a hint of defensiveness. "We didn't intend anything. Alexi and I discussed it a few times, but since no one asked, we didn't feel the need to advertise it. I've searched for cases of university professors and therapists disciplined for having affairs with students. I believe Alexi and I would be judged in a similar vein."

The meeting continued for another half hour—a palpable sadness interwoven with support for Alexi and Ellie.

Ellie's voice softened as she wrapped things up. "I'll email everyone tomorrow to give a heads-up that Friday's meeting will be brief—and a bit different." She offered an uneasy grin. "Alexi will clarify in an email for those unable to attend."

Alexi's gaze swept the room, a warm, grateful energy radiating from her. "Your unwavering support has been my anchor. Some of you have been attending these meetings for six years—I know I have." She smiled faintly.

"Maybe it's time for a break. Over the years, we've become a caring family, working together and building amazing friendships. It's been an incredible journey, and I'll miss you all. But with every ending, there's a new beginning."

She stopped, the twinkle in her eyes returning. "Did I just use that tired old cliché?"

Laughter broke the tension. They shared hugs and words of gratitude. Yet, beneath it all, there was a quiet sadness—the sense of being adrift without the spiritual guide who once led their way.

Chapter 54

Last Supper

The kitchen was buzzing with the clatter of dishes and the aroma of turkey. Mira beamed across the table. "Do you know how wonderful it feels to have Sunday dinner together every week?"

Lyam and Alexi glanced up from their bowls of leftover Christmas turkey soup and exchanged a smile. With a cheerful flourish, Alexi lifted her wine glass. "Absolutely! Salud, to fam dinners!"

Once the meal wound down, they drifted into the living room, settling into their usual seats that seemed to remember their shapes. Lyam leaned back and looked over at Alexi. "How are you holding up these days?"

Alexi paused, "Good question. How is Alexi doing? Usually, I'm the one asking this question when someone is going through a crisis. I remind them that what they're facing is like an upsetting scene in a movie. Now it's Ellie and me in the middle of the drama. "Ellie and I talked about ending things before the whole Abel mess. Maybe he was chosen to deliver the coup de grâce."

"But ending it this way! It seems so unfair," Mira chimed in.

Alexi shrugged with a half-smile. "Well, Mom, I'm 33—the same age Jesus was. At least tonight's not our Last Supper."

Lyam chuckled at their interchange and asked, "So, you're okay with no more meetings?"

"I'm so okay," Alexi nodded with a sense of comfort. "I'm not attached to the Friday meetings and never expected them to last this long. It was a good run, but after six years, I'm glad it's ending, instead of going a season too long, like *The Office*. Honestly, stepping off the stage feels like a breath of fresh air. Being in the spotlight changed how I connected with people. The only ones I felt normal around were you, Mira, and Ellie. It felt like most looked at me, wondering, 'What makes Alexi so special?' And in a way, it sort of did, even though I know no one is. A little crazy, yeah?"

"Crazy is an excellent word," Lyam agreed. "Like Kay telling Arlo, being special is no fun. You're handling this much better than I did when Alice took Mira from the rez. That was a complete meltdown for me. But it's like what Nietzsche said, 'What doesn't kill us, makes us stronger.'"

"Interesting! I forgot he said that." Alexi paused, filing the quote away in her mind. But her thoughts circled back to the meetings and her friends. *Was I truly helping, or just a crutch in their search to answer Who Am I?—the question at the core of it all. Sooner or later, they'll see that the one asking the question, is in fact, the answer.*

Refocusing on Lyam, she asked, "So, how did you snap out of it?"

"Snap out of it," Lyam chuckled. "I like that. After years of wallowing in self-pity and resenting Alice, I finally broke free. And it wasn't some pious act of mercy that turned the tide—it was a simple pair of scissors."

"Scissors?" Mira interjected.

"Once, while ballooning," Alexi explained, "Lyam told me about using imaginary scissors to cut loose judgments and grudges. I'll tell you more about that later."

Lyam's voice softened. "Then Kay came into my life. She guided me through the next steps, helping me shed my cocoon and showed me the power of relationships. Because of her, I had the desire to reconnect with Mira. A year after Kay died, an angel flew down from the sky and showed me the way."

"An angel in a Cessna?" Mira asked with a wry smile.

"Yes, Charlie," Lyam replied.

After a moment, he turned to Alexi. "Will you miss anything about the meetings?"

"Most definitely," Alexi said. "My friends, for sure. I'll also miss the shared energy in the room. It helped me find the right words, as if they were floating in the air, waiting for me to pluck them. I've always loved words, but our meetings showed me their true power. At the right moment, the right word is like an arrow pointing to where someone needs to look."

"Do you think you might ever have meetings again?" Mira asked.

Alexi shrugged, "Recreating that magic would be a tall order. Jill sees the ending as a tragedy and feels we should continue. But after Abel's email to the group?" She raised her eyebrows. "The reactions were mixed. Some were supportive, a few called me a charlatan, and the rest… well, anyone's guess."

She exhaled, "It stings, sure, but Ellie and I have no regrets. As George Harrison said, *All Things Must Pass*. I feel life's telling me to slow down and reset. I've been so focused on moving forward that I lost sight of what Kay told Arlo—about listening to your inner self."

Alexi paused, adding a shrug, "Anyway, Julie said she was going to hold monthly meetings using the tapes we started three years ago. So, in a way..."

As the room chilled, Lyam brought a steaming pot of tea from the kitchen. The warm scent of ginger filled the air as he poured and glanced at Alexi. "Last time Mati was in the shop, he mentioned his dream of riding from Alaska to Argentina is on hold because his partner got a job offer he couldn't refuse."

"Are you fishing?" Alexi grinned. "I have yet to tell Mom. But even before this whole thing, Mati asked me to ride with him, and now it's a done deal. But we're not riding tip to tip—we'll start from St. Cloud."

"Well, that's news," Mira raised an eyebrow. "I'm not sure how I feel about this. How long will it take?"

"We're not chasing a Guinness record. We plan to leave this spring, ride to Costa Rica, and fly back for Christmas the first year."

"The first year?" Mira's voice jumped a notch.

"The whole trip will take about two years—there are a lot of beaches along the way." Alexi's smile faded. "I'll miss being away from you and Lyam, but I'm also excited to start a new chapter in my life."

"Your ability to amaze me never ceases," Mira shook her head as Lyam and Alexi shared a laugh.

"Mati has always been a solid support, especially these past few weeks. Did I mention his parents live in Argentina? We'll ride from 'mi casa a su casa.'"

"Well, even I must admit, that's pretty cool." Mira smiled.

"He's been teaching me Spanish and Argentine Tango, so our trip will be fun in many ways. It's always been easy with him on our bike trips. I'm looking forward to this adventure, but it's more than the bike trip. I started writing another book, and riding inspires me."

"The rise and fall of a guru?" Mira teased.

"A serious book about the meetings over the last six years—without the drama. No one wants to read about that."

"But maybe some do," Mira added thoughtfully.

"Maybe, but they won't hear it from me."

After a brief pause, Lyam turned to Alexi. "I've never been

out of the country. Maybe Mira and I could join you for part of the ride south of the border?"

"Well, you know how I'd feel about that!" Alexi's voice bubbled. "And Mati thinks so highly of you—he'd be thrilled too."

Mira smiled, happy to be included. Memories of Mati's and Alexi's playful banter and laughter over dinner echoed in her mind. The idea of them becoming more than friends sparked her curiosity, but before she could dwell on it, Lyam gently cut in.

"How's Ellie these days?"

Alexi's expression softened. "I'm glad you asked. Ellie is a powerful and talented woman. She's been involved with our local Sierra Club for years. Last year, the main office in Oakland offered her a position, which happens to be close to where her parents live."

Alexi's smile was bittersweet. "Interestingly, she had her astrological chart read recently and was told she had a strong pull for family and kids. When she protested, the astrologer said, 'I tell you for certain it is true.' She'll be fine. We both agree that Abel was a truth stick for us. We know it's over, and we both feel a little relieved—and a whole lot of sad."

The three sat together in a comfortable, almost sacred silence, each quietly reflecting on their journey together. Their eyes met—a silent recognition of all they'd shared, the secrets uncovered, and the bond that had grown between them. After a moment, Mira exhaled softly, a hint of a smile on her lips.

"More tea? Pie?"

Acknowledgments

Thanks to Joseph Machney for contributing the two songs in this book.

Stay Connected

If you'd like to share your comments or help shape Book II of Alexi's continuing story, please email the author at:

AlexiWhoAmI@gmail.com

www.ingramcontent.com/pod-product-compliance
Lightning Source LLC
LaVergne TN
LVHW011219080426
835509LV00005B/215

* 9 7 8 1 4 2 1 8 3 5 8 4 6 *